ACTION SP
LOUDER THAN WORDS

*What coaching can do for your business -
17 Business Owners tell their stories.*

By

BRADLEY J. SUGARS
With
Grant McDuling

ACTION International Pty Ltd

ISBN 0958093253
FIRST EDITION

Published by *ACTION International* Pty Ltd
GPO Box 1340 Brisbane, QLD 4001
Phone: +61 (0) 7 3368 2525
Fax: +61 (0) 7 3368 2535
www.action-international.com

Distributed by *ACTION International* for further information
contact +61 (0) 7 3368 2525

Printed in Australia by Pure Print

This book is dedicated to all ACTION Business Coaches,
you are an amazing team.

■ Acknowledgments

I'd like to thanks all the business owners who agreed to let me write about their successes in business. It's never easy telling it warts and all for all the world to see. Their stories are an inspiration and will give countless others encouragement as they too pursue their dreams and goals.

I'd also like to thank the ACTION Business Coaches who put forward their clients for inclusion in this book. They are the ones that made it happen. They, like their clients, are reaping the rewards of their dedication and hard work.

■ CONTENTS

▌ Introduction

---

*If you don't drive your business,
you will be driven out of business.*

~ B. C. Forbes ~

Everyone likes to succeed in life. Whether it's at sport, education or business, success is what we all aim for. Yet not everyone succeeds at success.

Strange as it may seem, it's simple to succeed. You see, we're all born with the same amount of potential and brainpower. When things begin to go wrong, it's usually due to factors that have nothing whatsoever to do with what it takes to succeed.

Bad luck, being at the wrong place at the wrong time, not being clever enough, not having a 'business brain' or not having enough capital, are reasons too often bandied around. What rubbish.

You are what you are today because of the sum total of your actions. If you want a different result, you've got to do things differently. But you already know that, because if you didn't, you wouldn't have bought this book.

So congratulations on taking the first step to changing your lot in life. Congratulations on doing something positive – on deciding to accept accountability for your own future.

The formula for success in business is simple. And it's easily achievable. You can have anything you want, as long as you want it badly enough. Success is here in abundance, and there's more than enough to go around. All you have to do is want it badly enough, and then decide what you have to do to have it. The choice is yours.

But don't let me go on and on about this. After all, I have more than enough of everything that I've ever wanted to last many lifetimes. Listen instead to what others have to say. Listen to what ordinary businesspeople, just like you, have to say about the secrets to their success. And listen well. You don't have to re-invent the wheel, you know.

∎ The Case For A Coach

*The secret of business is to know something
that nobody else knows.*

~ Aristotle Onassis ~

Everyone knows, and accepts, that sporting stars need coaches. Without them they simply wouldn't succeed. Yet in most cases the coach isn't as good a player as the person being coached. And these coaches probably never reached the same heights of greatness either, but that doesn't detract from the need for a coach.

Even leading politicians and government department heads are surrounded by teams of advisors. It would be inconceivable not to have them. Every successful actor works under the watchful eye of an accomplished director, and the world's best musicians still follow the dictates of a conductor.

So what is it about business people? Why don't they, as a matter of course, have Business Coaches?

Well, this is now changing, with more and more business people realising that in today's fast-paced business environment, there's no way they can stay abreast of developments, let alone ahead of them. The case for a Business Coach has become unassailable. Well, to those serious about success, it has.

And it's no shame to have to accept the critique of an outside business expert – people in business have been listening to the advice of others for ages. Only it's usually been from the wrong people. Family, friends and colleagues have all featured prominently as 'confidants', but at what cost?

You see, the fact of the matter is that if you model your business on someone else's, chances are you'll reap the same results they did. Let's put it this way: If you want to bake a different cake, you need to use a different recipe. It's no good using someone's success secrets or tips, and then expect to get different results to that which they achieved. If you want to model yourself on someone – many do, and it's a sound philosophy – to at least choose a winner! Why model yourself on an ordinary person? And equally, why model your business on a mediocre one?

But there's another important factor to bear in mind, and that's objectivity. When you're running a company, it's very difficult to get an objective and honest answer to a problem from yourself. You've invariably got vested interests that sway your thinking. Pet likes and dislikes too, can ruin the best-intended business plans.

The Case For A Coach

Business owners these days tend to spend far too much time working IN their business rather than ON it. It's probably always been that way. However, to succeed, this has to change. It's the single biggest impediment to success that I've come across in all the thousands of companies I've worked with. Yet it's understandable. You see, when the vast majority of business owners first dreamed the dream of 'going it alone', they ventured out into the world of business by sticking to their field of expertise. A hairdresser opened a hairdressing salon, a motor mechanic opened a mechanical workshop and a printer opened a printing business. Sounds logical enough, but the reality is all they achieved was buying themselves another job. And one in which they would be destined to work longer and harder than ever before, and for little or no financial reward. It sounds crazy, and it is. That's because they end up working IN the job instead of ON the business.

It would have been far more sensible had that aspiring businessperson opened a business in which they had no previous experience or expertise. Sounds crazy? Absolutely not. They would then have had no option but to work ON the business, relying instead on the expertise of team members who would actually DO the work. This is one secret of success.

Sounds too simple? Then read on. This book is about ordinary business people achieving astonishing results through business coaching. It's all about stepping back, taking a good hard look at their business, then setting some very definite personal and business goals, and appointing a coach to get them there. Understand this; the coach is the only person who can see the forest for the trees. It's the coach who'll ensure you stay focused on the game, who'll make you run more laps than you thought you could (or should), and who'll tell it like it is. The coach is also the only person you can hire who'll act like your marketing manager, sales director, training co-ordinator, partner, confidant, mentor and best friend – all rolled into one.

Does having a coach guarantee you'll achieve success? The answer is NO, and for a very good reason. You see, although the coach will be there to guide you every step along the way, it's still you that will have to take to the field and play the game. It's your business, after all. You've got to actually do the work, because you're the only one who can be truly accountable. And when you get there, success will be all the sweeter for it.

It's all about accountability. This is such an important concept to understand, because it's fundamental to achieving success, not only in your business life, but in your private life as well. And it's something that should remain constantly in the forefront of your mind. It's so important I'm going to spend some time putting it into perspective.

Let's get imaginative for a while. Imagine there's a line that separates people into two basic categories. Think of it as a horizontal line.

People live their lives – and it can be their business or private lives – below the line or above it.

The first thing those who live below line do is to BLAME other people. They come up with EXCUSES. They DENY what they are doing or what is going on is their fault. They blame the economy for their poor performance in business, they use their difficult boss as an excuse for their lack of progress, or they deny their marriage break-up had anything to do with them. If this sounds like you, it means you are a VICTIM.

Those who play above the line say, "OK, let's take OWNERSHIP of our situation. Let's take RESPONSIBILITY for our actions ... let's be ACCOUNTABLE. If you play above the line, you're basically taking responsibility for your life. You're saying you're accountable for your results. You're saying you're not a VICTIM; you're a VICTOR. You're saying you're in charge of your life.

You might be surprised to learn that 95% of people live their lives below the line. Most just bumble along blaming others for their lot in life, and living their life in denial. If you want to succeed, you've got to shift into the zone above the line. That may take a quantum leap in your belief patterns. It may also require you to challenge the way you view life. But do whatever it takes. Take control of your life; assume the responsibility, and you'll be amazed at how you suddenly start making progress towards achieving the things you previously only ever dreamed of.

One other key point to achieving success is allowing yourself to fail every now and then. Allow yourself to make mistakes. If it's not OK to fail or make mistakes, you won't try new things. Instead, every time you try something new, you'll throw your hands up and say, "Wow, that's far enough. Don't go any further." The ability to fail is the sign of a true leader.

Remember, perfection leads to pain. Strive for excellence instead. This, of course, is something we are all ill-equipped for, as it's something that's not even touched on at school or university. We are not trained to succeed in business.

To succeed in business, we need to radically change the way we think. You see, our current education system is geared towards producing SPECIALISTS. But to succeed in business, you need to be a GENERALIST. Let me explain ...

Henry Ford knew one of the secrets to true entrepreneurial success. It's a common sense secret that is the opposite of everything we're taught as a specialist employee.

"When I need to know about finance, I call in my finance manager and ask him all the questions I need to have answered. The same goes for any other subject," Ford said.

In other words, the smartest leaders in the world employ specialists who are smarter than they are.

Henry Ford knew what every great entrepreneur knows ...

The Case For A Coach

Being an entrepreneur is about becoming a generalist, rather than a specialist.

A specialist (often known as an employee) is easily replaceable. A specialist is taught to follow. A specialist ends up working for a living, rather than living a life.

Let me explain …

Working in a job, you have about 1/3rd of your pay taken off in taxes, about 1/3rd taken to pay your mortgage or rent and even more to pay for your car(s) and so on. Eventually you've got just enough left over to EXIST on.

Generalists, on the other hand, think for themselves. They are great leaders, they take on the risks and reap the rewards from things like tax deductions, and, more importantly, they collect long-term income from the work they do today and every other day. They also enjoy the profits, as well as so much more.

The generalist, the person I refer to as the entrepreneur, works today to make money for the long-term. They work to build wealth rather than make income.

In school, we're taught to learn exactly what we're told, how we were told it, and when we were told it. Plus, you get good grades as long as you repeat it back in your tests exactly as it was taught in the books.

Even teachers are taught to follow the system. In the military every soldier is taught to follow orders. Only the GENERAL(ist) is taught to think for himself and to make decisions.

In the business world, employees are taught to acquire higher and higher levels of education, to specialize, to work hard, and to make enough income to pay their taxes, the mortgage, and then to exist until retirement.

True entrepreneurs, on the other hand, are required to be generalists, to think a lot and work a little, to take profits, write off expenses before paying taxes, and live the life of their dreams.

In the truest sense of the word, generalists are leaders. They live by the ideal that it's better to have 1% of one hundred people's efforts than 100% of their own.

Becoming a generalist is the first major task of anyone considering venturing into business for himself or herself.

It's the single biggest mindset change all employees who want to start their own businesses must make. Being the best at your trade, your profession or your job in no way means that you'll succeed in the world of entrepreneurial business. In fact, this is often the biggest hindrance to the success of most businesses.

Making this mindset change isn't easy – it involves radically altering the very way you think and perceive. Yet it must be done. And it must be maintained when attempted. Like quitting smoking, you can do it on your own, but it's very, very difficult. Much better to do so with professional help. Business is no different. You can go it alone, or you can do it so much quicker and with more certainty with a Business Coach. The choice is yours.

▌ Learning By Example

Example is the school of mankind,
and they will learn at no other.

~ Edmund Burke ~

Remember the saying **Do as I say, not as I do**? Well, that's the way of the traditional establishment. Rather it should be just **Do as I do**. That's how it always was in the old days. The real old days. Let me explain.

In feudal times, the leader of each clan was, to put it bluntly, the biggest and strongest person around. Why? Simply because the biggest and strongest was able to physically make their point heard to anyone who might consider mounting a challenge. Things didn't change much in those days and any one leader could rule for a lifetime.

Business was also very simple then, as the stability of the leader and the unchanging nature of the times meant everyone knew their place in life. Most people were content just to keep on producing over their very short life spans.

That was until the spear was invented.

Now, technology began to have an impact on the group. The most proficient spear-user became the potential new leader. Then the bow and arrow came along, followed by body armour. This development necessitated the invention of an even more sophisticated weapon – the gun.

The most effective user of this new technology (the bow and arrow, the gun, etc.) could now quite easily become the new leader.

As more and more inventions came to pass, and more and more products hit the marketplace, business and staying in charge, began to tax the minds of the leaders.

Here's where it all gets interesting … the leaders realized one very important fact - If they were to stay on as leader, they needed to 'think hard' rather than 'work hard'.

You see, if the leader was the smartest, as well as the biggest, person around, something truly extraordinary happened. The leader enrolled the inventors, those who knew things the leader didn't, as employees.

Learning By Example

The leaders now made sure these spears were only made for them; the guns were only made for them. As a result, another amazing thing happened.

The leader taught each employee to be a Master Specialist. He then encouraged his Master Specialists (nowadays known as Master Craftsmen) to take on apprentices, so they could teach other people to specialize in the same skills. These apprentices learnt by closely watching what the Master Specialist did and how he did it. The Master Specialist became the apprentice's mentor, and this system has worked very well through the centuries. It's still the way apprentices learn their trades today.

But the problem crept in when society moved from being predominantly agrarian-based to one that was largely industrial-based. The leaders, or white-collar workers, turned away from the mentor system towards a more academic system of learning. The motto here was **do as you're told**, with the emphasis being on repeating, parrot-fashion, as much as possible. Schools were built to teach people from early in life how to be good, how to do as they were told, how to fit into society and how to get a good job *(as a Specialist)*.

The mentor system had long-since gone out the window. The lessons of history had all but been forgotten.

Luckily all this seems set to change as more and more business people, the world over, are realising the advantages of watching and following the example of successful businesses. They are re-discovering the mentor system. They are learning that if a system works for one business, it should work for others. And they are seeing for themselves that they don't have to blunder around in the dark trying to reinvent the wheel – all they need to do is find a successful mentor and learn by example.

So how do you find other successful businesses to emulate? How do you discover who has a winning formula? After all, business people are notorious for playing their cards close to their chests. It's a competitive business they're in and it's often a case of the survival of the fittest. You can't just walk into the office of a prosperous-looking company and ask the owner if you can go through their accounts or take a look at their marketing and business plan.

That's where this book comes in. Read about the experiences of real business people and how they've overcome some of their most challenging issues. These are their own accounts, written largely in their own words. See for yourself how they've turned the seemingly impossible into the easily achievable. Marvel at how they've transformed struggling businesses that were nothing more than millstones around their necks into thriving entities that are now the envy of many.

And best of all, you'll begin to understand that if you learn from their experiences, your business can also flourish beyond your wildest dreams.

So let's go and visit some businesses that have done just that. We'll start with Tim Roberts' business, The Club Shoppe.

▌ Men's Clothing Store Increases Profit By 600%

---

*Anybody can cut prices, but it takes brains
to produce a better article.*

~ *P. D. Armour* ~

The Business

Name: The Club Shoppe

Address: Shop 47 – 48 St. Ives Shopping Village, St Ives NSW, Australia

Director/Owner: Tim and Natasha Roberts

Business Sector: Retail, Menswear

Purchased: 1999

Coach: Greg Albert

The Challenge

When Tim and Natasha bought their business, they set themselves a few goals that they thought were reasonable. They wanted to make the business profitable, and to increase turnover by 50% and profit by 70%. To put this in perspective, they thought that if they could make a total profit of $150,000, they'd be more than happy. They also wanted to pay $150,000 off their business loan and to be in a position to hire a new team member.

Of course, they also set themselves some personal goals such as being able to spend more time with the family, to earn enough to landscape the backyard, and to get focus and direction back into their lives.

So how did they feel on purchasing the business? Instead of feeling elated, they felt lost, and instead of feeling self-satisfied, they felt trapped – hardly what they expected on achieving their dream of owning their own business.

To make matters worse, the business had a severe cashflow problem when they bought it. It had too much inventory tied up. Profitability was low and discounting normal.

Like many, they decided to keep the original owner on in an effort to make a smooth transition, and they felt reluctant to try anything new. There was no loyalty program in place and no real communication with clients. It became blatantly obvious that their best marketing efforts had not worked.

It was not a fun place to be, and the atmosphere could be described as dull, at best. They spent their days just waiting for clients to walk in.

Now that you have a basic understanding of the situation facing Tim and Natasha, let's hear the details from Tim. This will give you a very good understanding of what he went through in facing-up to the challenges that lay before them. It will also give you an idea of how important it is to take responsibility for your situation, in being able to recognise the signs and to take positive steps to put things back on track, so you can meet your longer-term goals.

Tim's Story

When I left school in 1989, I never in my wildest dreams thought I would end up in retail, let alone owning a business that sells menswear. In fact, before I bought The Club Shoppe in 1999, I knew absolutely nothing about menswear.

I actually started out as a School Teacher and although it's a noble profession, I discovered real early that it was not for me, and that it would not take me to where I wanted to go.

So with the help of my family, I decided to buy a business. In fact, it was a small music store that just happened to be situated next door to the menswear store that I would eventually buy. I was relatively successful with my music store, but had developed a passion for menswear, so I decided to go for it.

It would also be fair to say that prior to meeting my Business Coach, Greg Albert, in 2001, I knew very little about how to run a business effectively and profitably, although I never realised that at the time. In the 14 months that I followed Greg's lead, I have turned The Club Shoppe into a viable and profitable business that is now a lot of fun, an integral part of my life and a business with huge potential.

But I'm jumping ahead here. Let me start at the beginning ...

The Club Shoppe was established in 1959 by the then minister for the Environment, the Honourable Mr. Barry Cohen. Soon thereafter, Barry employed Ray Jacomb to manage the business whilst he pursued his political ambitions.

In the 35 years that followed, Ray turned The Club Shoppe into one of the finest menswear stores in the country, selling only the finest clothing available anywhere in the world.

When I bought the business, The Club Shoppe was operating just as it always had; very smoothly and generating good profit – or so I thought.

The shop is based on the north side of Sydney in an affluent suburb, and stocks the very top-end of men's fashion.

When I bought the business, I knew nothing about menswear. I didn't even know how to read a tape measure. However, I had an extremely good mentor in Ray, who, fortunately for me, had decided to stay on for another two years to teach me every aspect of the business.

I dedicated myself to learning the basics during the first 12 months. I was so determined to learn the business that I could not think of anything else. I lived and breathed the business, everything from how to sell a suit to ordering clothing for the new season. I literally drained Ray of information. You see, I was thirsty for information, and he was more than happy to give it to me.

After the first 12 months, however, I began to realise the business had a lot of flaws, and I noted that they were very serious flaws.

These included the following:

- At the beginning of every season, the business experienced very severe cashflow problems, which were impacted by the introduction of the GST. These problems arose from trying to find the cash for the duty/freight and GST on imported goods. Every season this amounted to over $100,000 - and it always materialised during the quietest times of the year (that is at the beginning of a season). Although we were making good profit, all of it was tied up in excess stock.

- Because The Club Shoppe was established in 1959 it had a very dedicated clientele … the problem was they were getting older. Many of the customers whom the shop was built around were retiring and no longer needed the expensive suit or a new range of casual clothing every season. I could see that for ten or so years the shop's turnover was stagnant, and did not rise or fall by more than thirty of forty thousand every year. I was worried that in ten years time I would not have a business left.

- For 40 years, the shop had been built around Ray, who would work more than 50 hours a week. Customers would come into the store looking for him and some would only come back when he was there. I was absolutely petrified of what would happen to the business when he decided to retire. Even though I had learnt extremely quickly and knew I could do everything he could, people still wanted Ray to look after them.

- The shop had developed something of a discount culture; we regularly gave discounts to our VIP's and we had numerous sales, which tended to attract the wrong type of customer – price shoppers – so our profitability was heading in the wrong direction.

- Although I did not know it at the time, I had become reliant on the 'old ways' of doing business. For the first 15 months I had a bookkeeper that looked after everything from paying bills to doing the banking. She was also, you might say, my own secretary. This was a big mistake. Although this bookkeeper did her work well, I never had a handle on the company's finances. I never knew the impact my cashflow problems were having on the business. I didn't even know how much I owed suppliers or how much I had in the bank at any one time. I realise now how silly I was at that time, but in hindsight, I was spending all my time in the shop concentrating on the physical aspects of selling.

After the first 12 months, the excitement of a new business was well and truly wearing off. The GST had been implemented and the Sydney Olympic Games was looming. Business was down, cashflow was pathetic and I felt absolutely trapped. What's more my wife Natasha had just delivered our first child and her maternity leave was about to run out. We had two choices: either she would go back to work or I'd have to build a place for her in the business. We chose the latter.

Natasha took charge of computerising all our accounts in the business. This turned out to be the first of many steps we took to turn the business around. And it was the first time that I could see every dollar being spent, and earned. I started to gain control of the business, and I really started to feel that it was mine. Our current bookkeeper decided to leave, and this gave Natasha and I real scope as far as the accounts were concerned. I could see that we were ordering too much stock. I also realised we had far too many suppliers.

Things began to improve, and by the end of that financial year, we actually made a nice little profit. I put this solely down to the fact that we had better financial management. However, I still felt trapped. I wanted to spend more time with my family, yet I felt tied to the shop. I was constantly under pressure to be there more.

The Moment Of Truth

It all changed one fateful night in September 2001. The centre management had invited a representative from **ACTION International** to do a free seminar on Sales and Marketing to show us how we could improve our businesses. I thought I would go along just to see what these 'consultants' were on about and what ideas they might have.

I thought it was all very weird when one of their representatives started trying to balance about ten helium balloons all at once. I was actually going to get up and leave.

Then it all changed. Greg Albert stood up and started to pull my strings. He asked the group how many of us were truly free of our businesses. How many of us could take days, weeks or months off whenever we wanted to. How many of us could be assured our businesses would run efficiently and effectively whether we were working or not. How many of us truly valued the concept of time, and how many of us were spending our time doing things we enjoyed, or would rather be doing something else.

Greg proceeded to tell us all about **ACTION International** and the options that were available in their **ACTION** Plan. I took the information home and told Natasha about my evening. I remember going to sleep thinking, "I dare you to give it a try."

The very next day, I did.

I gave Greg a call and the rest, for me, is history.

On my first meeting with Greg, he asked, "What is it that you want most of all from your business?" At that stage my sights were limited. I knew Natasha wanted our backyard landscaped, so I replied, "I want the business to earn enough money so we could get our backyard landscaped."

Greg smiled wryly and asked, "OK, so we are in September, what do you want from the business in October?"

I'd never really thought about it before, but Greg kept asking questions, delving deeper and deeper. It all really came down to one thing: time. I began to realise this was the commodity I wanted most.

I wanted to spend time with my family; time to do whatever I wanted, when I wanted. I didn't want to feel trapped and full of worry.

I'm sure you have all heard the saying, "Spend more time working ON the business, not IN it." I never really understood that until I started working with Greg. For the first 3 months, that's what Greg taught me to do. I systemised everything in the business, from opening up the shop, to how to measure up a client for a suit, to how to manage the computerised Point of Sale System. This seemed at the time an extremely tireless job, however, I absolutely loved it. I could see that it was the first step toward building a better business.

It wasn't long before I could afford to spend a day at home each week working on the business. This totally re-energised me and I began to think, "Hey, this can really work for me."

Greg taught me that consistency was the key to a successful business. It was also the key to releasing myself from working IN the business and spending more time working ON the business. You see, if a customer were to come into the shop, he or she must experience the same level of service no matter who served them. And they must have exactly the same experience every time they came in.

This was my first step to making the business less reliant on Ray, and also on me.

We started a VIP program and set about signing up our key A-grade clients. We then began holding special events every month. But what we needed most, at the time, was to make some quick cash.

In October of 2001, I had my first taste of a successful marketing campaign, and what an absolute eye opener it was. Once we had our new stock in for that season, we experienced our first success. Greg suggested we hold a closed-door sale for my loyal customers. So I invited them to an event to celebrate the arrival of our new season's stock. We served refreshments and gave anyone who spent in excess of $1,500 a dinner at one of Sydney's most exclusive Italian restaurants.

I must admit that I did have certain expectations and hoped for a good turn up, but never in my wildest dreams did I think I'd get the turn up we did.

In one weekend we took more than what we typically would in 10 days of trading. After the event, Ray said, "In my 37-years in this business, I have never ever experienced anything quite like it!" What was even better was the fact that our takings were on full margin; there were no discounts given and nothing was 'on sale'. That day we gave out 13 dinners to the value of $150 each.

I had started. I was now really hungry for more.

All of a sudden, instead of just plodding along and wishing for customers to come through the door, I proactively went after them. I started a frequent buyer's programme that rewarded customers every time they bought, with points that could be redeemed at a later stage for goods from the shop.

I began to compile specific customer lists that grouped people together according to their likes and dislikes. This enabled me to plan promotions for each individual group and to make contact with them specifically. For example, I organised a 'Made to Measure' suit and jacket promotion and was able to reach my target market because I had a list of people who had an interest in Made to Measure articles. When we received new merchandise from particular labels such as Polo Ralph Lauren, I had a list of people whom I knew wanted to be told about it.

I organised an agreement with Lavazza Coffee whereby I would serve their coffee to our customers, if they supplied me the coffee and an espresso machine free of charge. I also had wine and whiskey for those customers who had had a particularly difficult day at work. And do you know what? Some customers began coming in just to say hello and to have a cuppa. It was great.

I even recently invited the local Harley Davidson dealer to put a bike on display in the shop. It was great to see these 'shopped-out' husbands dragging their wives into the store to see the Harley, and to hear their wives say, "Yeah sure, but you need some new clothes!" Work was becoming really fun.

Greg warned me that other shop owners would think I was a bit weird. I remember once when centre traffic was slow, the other shop owners were complaining how slow business was. I was booming. They kept asking me how I did it, and I always said, "Get a coach." It amazed me that no one took my advice.

In the first 6 months of working with Greg, our turnover increased by 18%, but more importantly, our profit increased by nearly 40%. I was hooked. I have never enjoyed working so much.

When it came time for our next season's launch, I wanted to try something a little different. However, I didn't know what. One day I was speaking to Greg about the latest James Bond movie and he said, "Wouldn't it be great if we could get James Bond into the store for the promotion."

Well, unfortunately Pierce Brosnan was busy that weekend, but I organised for an Aston Martin DB7 to be on display in the shop instead. I also organised complimentary dinners at the MG Garage Restaurant for our customers. Well, that promotion was even more successful than the first.

What I really enjoyed most of all was hearing compliments from our customers like, "There is no other store that offers me as much as what you do," and "You know you are ruining my overseas shopping experiences, because I just come here for everything now." Then there was this: "My husband keeps telling me to ask you to stop having promotions, because he enjoys coming here for them and always spends too much money."

I love these comments. It makes me think I'm doing something right. I mean I love communicating with my customers, and if they leave feeling happy, then I know I have done something right.

We basically changed the business from being a passive one (waiting for customers to turn up) to one that is a real fun place; one that is an incredible experience. This concept is breathtakingly simple, yet difficult for owners who are store-blind to see.

Go the extra mile. That is what Greg keeps telling me. We do things that I can guarantee nobody else does. Like sending new customers thank you gifts for coming into our shop, whether they buy anything or not. Or sending our good customers gifts like pen sets or calculators.

I remember one instance when a lady came into our store and began looking around. I introduced myself and struck up a conversation. She had never been into our store before, even though she was a local. She told me that her husband shopped at one our competitors about 20 km away. I took her address and her husband's name. When she left, I boxed up a pen and pencil set that we had purchases for our good customers and promptly sent it to her. That weekend she and her husband came into the shop and spent over $6,000. They are now dedicated customers.

"If you have to make a decision, make it in favour of the customer," Greg would say to the team. My team were becoming so good, it did not matter who served our customers. What a change.

I was able to promote my young salesperson to general manager. I then recruited another team member to train, Ray was able to semi-retire, and I got to spend time with my family; we were all progressing towards realising our own dreams.

One of the advantages of having a more successful business was that I managed to afford to increase the size of our store by 30 square metres, and I spent $50,000 fitting it out. Needless to say during the refit, (funny how it always seems to take longer than expected) our turnover was not good. Consequently I decided to get in some ties for a promotion. Once the refit was completed, I sent out a letter to all our customers offering them a free tie just for coming to have a look at the new shop. Over a 3-day period I gave away 23 ties (at the value of $11 each) and I took in over $23,000.

I still have a very long way to go in the business. In fact, I feel I have only just begun. My next step is to build the business to a stage where I could franchise it to begin making some passive income.

I am currently not only enjoying working in my business, but I also absolutely love the extra time I have with my young family. If that's all I ever achieve in life, then my time with Greg has been worthwhile.

I have gone from a position of negative cashflow, negative profits, working long hours, and questionable customer loyalty to owning a company that is thriving.

Oh, and Greg managed to get our backyard make-over money in one weekend! I am so glad I got into *ACTION*!

The Coach's Story

At first, Tim was very sceptical. However, he was in such a situation that he was willing to give Business Coaching a go. To begin with, he found the initial telephone coaching call not as effective as a face-to-face meeting (he's a real people's person) but soon realised that it was more focused and productive.

Tim's a great client. He's very eager to learn, has an open mind and a desire to do whatever it takes. No matter how arduous the task or weird the suggestion, he would grab it with both hands and give it a go.

Tim's core values are aligned with those of *ACTION*, especially concerning rewarding customers and the team. Consequently, all strategies were painlessly implemented.

I started with an Alignment Consultation to get real clear on the goals and challenges. I then got him to read several books while an Action Plan was being prepared.

I started with the basics. This included preparing a cashflow forecast and developing a plan of action to swing this into positive territory. We then increase prices, stopped all discounting, and reduced costs, including the inventory. We negotiated better terms with suppliers. A team incentive plan was instituted. Simple routines were systemised. We measured various business activities and taught sales skills. Conversion rates (from prospects to clients) were monitored and measured. Scripts were introduced. We then established exclusive lines, created package deals, started a VIP program and established events that we marketed to our VIP's every month. The first was a highly successful closed-door sale. We ran an off-premises old stock clearance, and set up numerous strategic alliances. Critical non-essentials were introduced. I then began training the team to build Raving Fans, and introduced programs to keep customers for life. A new recruitment system for new team members was also introduced.

I'm pleased to report that the owner is now able to spend 1 full-day a week working ON the business (developing strategies, etc.) and has prepared clear budgets and targets, both monthly and weekly, that the team are monitored against.

The Outcome

After 3 months, the owner was spending 1 day a week less at work. He re-evaluated the team and introduced testing and measuring, as well as sales training. Their conversion rate increased from 50% to 70%. Discounting is now a thing of the past. Prices have actually been increased, and profit has gone from negative to +11%.

After 6 months, cashflow forecasts indicated an inventory challenge. This was tackled with new contracts put in place and 'dead' stock cleared. The conversion rate was now better than 80%. A 10% increase in profit per month became our target. A new key team member was employed when an existing salesperson was promoted to General Manger, freeing up the owner. 500 people were enrolled in the VIP program. They then secured the distribution rights for Brioni and Paul Smith suits, and introduced Made To Measure in Milan and Zegna suits. Turnover increased by 10%, with profit up 40%.

After 12 months the owner is able to go on holidays whenever he wants too. The business now only services A-grade clients and does not cater for price-shoppers or discount hunters at all. The store has a fun, happy and professional atmosphere. A hire business is ready to launch. Turnover is up by 12%, and profit up by 600%. The business is now cashflow positive. Business systems are in place and the owner is looking at multiple outlets.

▌ Graffiti Removal Business - From Smallest To Biggest In 6 Years

---

Business is more exciting than any game.

~ Lord Beaverbrook ~

The Business

Name: First Choice Protective Coatings

Address: 1/133 Carnegie Place, Blacktown, NSW, 2148, Australia

Director/Owner: Scott and John Paterson

Type Of Business: Graffiti Removals, Anti-Graffiti Coatings, Pressure Cleaning and Painting

Business Sector: Cleaning, Building, Painting

Established: 1996

Coach: Greg Albert

The Challenge

The Paterson brothers came into this business from different routes – Scott from the world of optics and John from plumbing. Both could be regarded as fairly typical tradespeople, and neither had any real business expertise to speak of. They did, however, have something going for them. They were enthusiastic, dedicated and hard working. And they happened to stumble across a product they believed could sell well.

After 6 good years in business, the company had reached a plateau; they didn't know which direction to take next, and although they were doing quite well, they had reached a level where they were bogged down. Try as they might, they couldn't seem to grow the business.

They weren't making a profit, but they weren't losing anything either. And like most people in business, they had aspirations. They also realised that, with their lack of resources and knowledge, they wouldn't be able to take their business to the next level on their own. They acknowledged that they needed professional help.

Scott's Story

My previous experience is in optics. I worked as an Optical Mechanic and an Optical Dispenser for a period of 10 years. During that time, I had no experience in graffiti removal whatsoever, I also had no interest in the subject at all.

I thought my future was going to be in Optics. I could see myself moving up the corporate ladder, and this is something I wanted to do.

My brother John's background is plumbing. He's been a plumber all his life. He then moved into the wholesale side of the business and started a company that sold bathroom vanities, toilet suites, tapwares and that sort of thing. He spent his time wholesaling plumbing supplies to hardware stores.

Then one day this Chemist said to him, "When you're out selling your plumbing products, can you just go to hardware stores and see if you can sell my graffiti removal products?" John replied, "Oh yes, no worries." He took it on but nothing ever came of it.

His business struggled on for about 2 years until one day his partner left to move to Queensland, placing him in a bit of a predicament. He asked me if I would like to join him in the business. I thought about it long and hard before deciding to take a gamble. I thought if all else failed I could always go back to optics, as I'm qualified in more areas than most people and would therefore find it fairly easy to get a job.

I would give it 12 months, and if it didn't work out, I'd revert back to my old occupation. My wife wasn't very happy about it at all.

But I took the plunge and started selling plumbing products and hardware items. Even though our sales increased, we still had problems with our suppliers, making it difficult for us to supply our customers on a regular basis.

I began taking a closer look at the graffiti product and said, "Why don't we try to do something with it?"

Well, eventually we began selling three products: a Graffiti Remover liquid spray, a Graffiti Remover in gel form and a Sacrificial Anti-Graffiti Protective Coating.

We decided to make-up a few labels and began promoting the products to hardware stores and local councils. People were amazed as they had never really heard of anti-graffiti products before.

It started selling; hardware stores began putting it on their shelves and it was proving quite a success for us. The only problem was, people were buying it but not re-ordering, so we wanted to find out why.

Graffiti Removal Business - From Smallest To Biggest In 6 Years

We started putting our phone number on the labels. This generated calls from people asking us to remove graffiti for them, as they still weren't sure how to do it themselves. We also had no experience in removing graffiti ourselves. We were working out of John's home in Epping. It was a home office set-up, which wasn't really adequate at all. I was living at Seven Hills in Sydney's West; John was living in Epping, inSydney's North.

But once people started asking us to remove their graffiti, we thought we might as well give it a go. So we bought a little pressure cleaner and together with our little ute, we though we had it made. We thought this was the way to go – we could make decent money by providing a service and selling our products at the same time.

We began receiving more and more phone calls from clients. I then started searching the internet and found Holroyd Council had put out tenders looking for someone to clean their toilets and remove graffiti. We began debating whether we should do this or not. So we thought why not, we'd take a gamble - working hand-in-hand cleaning the toilets and removing the graffiti. We were the successful tenderer.

But we didn't know how to clean toilets either. We had an outline of what we were supposed to be doing, but we weren't too sure.

We started working about 18 hours a day, because toilets had to be cleaned after hours. We worked these hours for 18 months, not sure where we were going. We knew we were doing well, so we finally leased two new Holden Combos. We thought we were fantastic. We had the Combos sign-written, loaded them up with our anti-graffiti products and bought a little pressure cleaner each. We removed graffiti from Holroyd Council during the day, and at night we cleaned their toilets.

Then one weekend we were surfing the internet and came across another tender for graffiti removal from schools and railway stations for the Department of Public Works. We tendered and made the preferred supplier listing ranked 3rd. At first we picked up small jobs, because the other companies couldn't deliver. Then one day the preferred supplier folded and we moved up the ladder, which enabled us to get more work.

We decided the time had come to move out of the home office and a mate of John's, who owned a factory at Pendle Hill, asked if we would be interested in renting the rear of his factory. We went and had a look. It was dirty, run-down and had mould on the walls, so we cleaned it from head to toe. We fitted the cheapest carpet we could find, and made use of some old desks and chairs. But it was better than the home office and it was something we could call our own. The rent was very cheap; they looked after us and gave us help whenever we needed it.

After setting the office up, we applied for a central phone number, making out we were bigger than we actually were. People started taking us more seriously.

Graffiti Removal Business - From Smallest To Biggest In 6 Years

The business was growing more and more. We were still working 18-hour days, but we found with more and more work coming in, we just couldn't handle it. We knew we had to put someone on. We 'bit the bullet' and employed a friend. He already had his own ute, so all we had to do was supply him with pressure cleaners, hoses and product. We gave him some training, sent him out on his way and thought we were doing fantastically well.

At about this time, my pregnant sister, Heather, had just been made redundant. She used to come in 1 day a week to answer the phones. This soon became two days a week and now she is with us full-time.

Getting back to our 18-hour work days, we worked very hard, but we enjoyed what we were doing. We knew we couldn't go on like that for much longer, even though we had employed another person, so we decided to sub-contract out our toilet cleaning work, preferring instead to concentrate on the graffiti removal side of the business. We got rid of the Combos and upgraded to Holden Rodeo Dual Cabs. We were now going places. We had Holden Rodeos with canopies, tow bars, air conditioning, the whole lot. We thought we had actually made it.

Work started rolling in, so we decided to employ another person, again a family member. Everything was rosy and sweet. Business was going well – in fact, it was thriving. Public Works and Holroyd Council kept giving us more and more work. We decided to employ another person, which made 3 all up. With that also came another three cars, so we had 5 people on the road, including John and myself. I was out there removing graffiti during the day and taking my paperwork home at night.

I knew something had to give.

I decided to take myself off the tools for a couple of days each week just to concentrate on running the business and this proved quite successful.

We soon found that through working with Public Works and Holroyd Council, we began building quite a reputation for graffiti removal.

By the end of the 1999 financial year, the company actually made a net profit of

$70,000. We were stoked with that result and bought more machinery and planned to make some improvements. We also employed a casual. We diversified slightly, but still 98% of our work was contract work, which was secure. It was steady, reliable and we knew we were going to get paid.

After doing so well that year, I knew we could do even better but I didn't know how to go about it. I didn't know where we should be going, what we should be doing, what direction we should be taking, whether we should be taking more risks or even whether we should stay where we were.

The Moment Of Truth

We stagnated for the next 6 to 8 months. We weren't doing any better, but we weren't doing any worse either. Something kept worrying me as we had grown fairly fast until then. To go from a rapid growth-rate rate to suddenly standing still scared me. I began to wonder whether the company was actually in decline and started thinking that we should sell before it was too late. I began to think about looking for another job again, and wondered when I should start firing people.

I didn't know where to go for help, whom to turn to, or where to get advice, because I didn't have the business skills myself to answer the questions that I needed answered.

I was travelling home from work late one night, listening to the radio and thinking about the company, when I heard an *ACTION International* advertisement. It said they could help companies or businesses reach their next level, achieve their goals and provide financial freedom. This made me take notice, so I wrote down the number and thought I'd give them a call the next day.

The next morning I gave *ACTION International* a call. I spoke to Greg Albert, and told him of our situation. I said we felt as if we had stagnated and didn't know which direction to take. I wanted to get his advice and find out what he could actually do for our company.

Greg said he would start by sending us some testimonial tapes of other companies that had been successful with *ACTION International*, and I thought, "Oh yeah, here we go, bring out the tapes." I was fairly sceptical, but asked for the tapes anyway, as I was in dire straits and clutching at straws.

After receiving the tapes, I listened to them and read the literature that was sent. I must admit I was quite intrigued and hyped up after listening to these tapes. I thought they were very good. I actually rang Greg and told him I had listened to them and was quite impressed. We arranged to meet.

During that meeting, Greg sat and listened to our story, where we were going and what we actually did. I didn't realize until after the interview that what he was actually doing was just sitting back and taking it all in to find out where we were at and where our interests lay.

He then suggested we draw up a business plan. This involved looking at modules over a 3, 6, 9, 12, and 18-month period (or however long it took to find out exactly where we were at in our own company.) From marketing to our personal stuff, from business structures to administration; in fact everything from start to finish, including where we should be achieving results, where we had been achieving results, where we hadn't, and what we should actually be doing.

Even though I didn't realise it during the first interview, I actually had a great rapport with Greg. You feel a certain bond or something with that other person and you feel they can help you achieve certain results.

We signed up with Greg and **ACTION International**, and started our first module. At the end of each week, John, Heather and I would sit down together and work through the material, page-by-page, question-by-question. After going through each one, we pooled our answers to come up with the best result. That proved successful, as we often came up with similar answers.

After completing the modules, a process that took about 9 months, we received our draft plan. We noticed that many of our goals had actually changed from the time we originally began writing them down. We had actually grown so much during those 9 months it was incredible. Our attitude had actually changed and we had a clearer picture of where we should be heading.

We were quite happy and I thought this was a bit of a success for us.

We were sent our final business plan leather-bound with a priority listing of what we needed to do. We needed to pay immediate attention to our marketing strategies – to target more private customers. That's when Greg suggested that, seeing we had completed our business plan, we should commence weekly 1-hour coaching sessions whereby we'd talk over on the phone what we had actually done during the week. Each time we talked, Greg would suggest work we needed to do to complete our goals (in our business plan) and I would ask questions.

We went through this procedure every week, and Greg would come out to see us whenever he needed to. He also would come to our staff training days and spend a couple hours talking to the team. Not asking for anything extra, he truly just wanted us to succeed and to push us forward.

I'd just like to add that the Business Coach doesn't actually do the work for you. They don't even tell you what to do. You have to work out the answers for yourself. They'll guide you and push you, but you've got to do the work. I truly believe that this way you gain a lot more knowledge than if the coach were to simply tell you what was to be done. We had to learn to think for ourselves and work out how to do things we wouldn't normally do.

The Coach's Story

When I met Scott, John and Heather for the first time in a very small and dingy office, I wondered how I could help these people. They were a fairly typical trades-type company where they did everything themselves – there were no systems and they had no real team. But they had the desire to move beyond where they were at the time.

They never made excuses; they just asked, "What can we do?"

They were eager to learn. I felt it best to start with our Success Model Planning System, which would get them focused and clear, as they were a bit lost. This proved to be the best strategy. They grew so much through this 9-month process. They actually re-did certain modules as things became clearer. Scott was thirsty for knowledge and we really tried many different things, including some innovative marketing which was completely new to them.

Their first task was to solidify all functions in the business, build and train a real team and then increase the business. Increasing the business turned out to be fairly easy, which showed they had great potential in the market place.

It's fairly simple to be successful with trades-related companies; just solve whatever frustrations the customers have when dealing with that particular industry. This was the basis upon which we developed a very professional operation.

I have seen Scott and John grow immensely over the past two years. They are now very dedicated business owners, willing to try new things and continually going the extra mile. Never once during the planning or coaching sessions were they negative; never did they say this or that wouldn't work. They were open to new ideas, enjoyed trying new things and were always eager to gain more knowledge through coaching, external courses, or the books and tapes I recommended.

In 2002, they were awarded the title 'Best Small Business' in Blacktown – a fantastic effort. Scott now works ON the business, not IN it, and we are building the systems and support structure necessary to launch the Graffiti Off Franchise. Very exciting times indeed.

Scott now regularly establishes budgets and targets for the team, and knows his break-even point. He can now read and understand Profit and Loss Statements and Balance Sheets, something that was only done before by his accountant once a year. In fact, he previously never even looked at them!

The Outcome

Since the start of coaching, turnover has increased by 300% and profit by a whopping 600%. Future targets exceed even that. They have been in business now for 6 years and are still going strong.

Their goals are to franchise the company, first in the Sydney Metropolitan area, then within the state of New South Wales, before going national and international.

The owners also aim to work more on the business instead of in it. They also aim to become financially free and to have other business interests besides this company.

Graffiti Removal Business - From Smallest To Biggest In 6 Years

During their first year with **ACTION International**, they completed a business plan and doubled their profits. They have also bought a factory at Blacktown, and now have a boardroom, two offices upstairs, a lunchroom, an area for storage and a reception area downstairs. This is something that, at the end of the day, they can call their own. This has been all achieved by doing all the hard work themselves.

But not only hard work; a lot of smart work on the part of Greg Albert for helping them achieve these results. Moving into their factory in Blacktown has given them a new perspective on where they are heading and what they are actually doing.

They also underwent changes as far as their team was concerned. Some of their team didn't like the changes that were taking place; the owners were probably stricter and the company was structured better. These people have since departed and a new team with very clear guidelines as to what their role within the company is, and who fit in with their new structure, has been established.

The company is now running very smoothly with high work ethics, high morale and everyone is working towards achieving the same goals. Each team member is rewarded for the input they provide.

The company now employs 11 team members. They have appointed an Operations Manager who oversees the day-to-day running of the company out in the field, while John is currently the C.E.O and Scott is working on franchising the business. They can now see more light at the end of the tunnel and this, they say, is going to be one of their greatest achievements.

First Choice Protective Coatings is now one of the largest Graffiti Removal companies in Australia. The owners say they have achieved a lot more than they would ever have hoped, thanks to Greg Albert and **ACTION International**. Their turnover is higher, their profits are higher, their morale is higher still and their business sense and knowledge has grown dramatically. And they've re-named the company Graffiti Off. They say this was very definitely money well spent.

One last thing; thanks to taking a Business Coach on board, Scott has brought his first luxury car, a beautiful Jaguar. For him, life's exciting, and it's fun.

▌From Small Pharmacy To International Franchise

---

*If you can run one business well,
you can run any business well.*

~ Richard Branson ~

The Business

Name: Health Information Pharmacy

Address: 269 Old Northern Rd, Castle Hill, Sydney, NSW, 2154, Australia

Director/Owner: Ken and Julia Lee

Type Of Business: Retail Pharmacy

Business Sector: Pharmaceutical Industry

Purchased: 1998

Coach: Greg Albert

The Challenge

Health Information Pharmacy is a retail pharmacy located right next door to a medical centre. It is situated away from a shopping centre, and it's a stand-alone business with hardly any traffic flow. Many of its customers are middle to high-income earners, families, some baby boomers and the elderly.

When Ken took over the pharmacy in October 1998 it looked tired and was run as a traditional pharmacy – there was very little delegation and the Pharmacist did everything. The business needed a good injection of business skills. It also needed merchandising to be introduced.

Ken's Story

At university, Ken says he was trained to be a pharmacist, not a business owner. Then once he'd qualified and begun working, he soon realised he needed to accelerate his business knowledge through coaching and mentoring. He also wanted to network with other businesses as a means of helping to improve his own.

The Moment Of Truth

After owning the pharmacy for 2 years, the Lee's moment of truth arrived with the possible deregulation of the pharmaceutical industry and the introduction of discounting. It became apparent that discounting had to be done in volume for the business to survive. So they decided against discounting, opting instead for a policy of adding value. This meant they needed help.

Ken had just read Brad Sugars' book *Instant Cashflow* and responded to an advertisement that *ACTION* Coach, Greg Albert had placed in the local newspaper.

When Ken and Julia first approached Greg, their initial goal was to try and free-up their time. They were working a 120-hour week between them. They wanted to leverage Julia out of the business first, and then Ken.

One of the challenges they faced was that the business was making a profit while they were working it, but it wouldn't if they stepped out. Obviously they wanted to change this, but they also wanted to create a business model that could be replicated through franchising.

Since teaming up with Greg and *ACTION*, the business has undergone a complete transformation. They created a business model that proactively takes responsibility for people's health, they developed values that are set in concrete, and they created a unique business around those values.

The core values of Health Information Pharmacy include the following:

- Reducing medication problems.

- Empowerment of people.

- Strengthening their community.

- Helping the less fortunate.

They started by doing an Alignment Consultation and setting goals (which have since changed, but were nevertheless a good start). They then embarked on a program of team training that improved their customer service levels exponentially, and developed a team incentive program called Teamaximiser™.

Teamaximiser™ is designed to give incentives to all team members based on their job description. Based on *ACTION's* 5 Ways Leverage Chart, it also encourages companion selling and the giving out of information, while allowing the owner to know what team members are doing every hour of the day. Team members are 'penalised' for not following sales scripts or coming to work late.

One of the keys to the success of Teamaximiser™ is that there are bonuses based on individual and team performances; therefore, team members are not just working for themselves but also for a common goal. This is powerful and works well, even without the owners being there. It has also proved highly successful at different sites.

The creation of a Unique Selling Proposition (USP) was also another system that came about through their work with **ACTION**. Chemconsult™ is now trademarked and is a unique pharmaceutical consulting process. The pharmacy USP fits in with the vision of the pharmacy, which is: *'Advice for a happier, longer and healthier life.'*

Through this system, Health Information Pharmacy is helping to improve patients' lives and keep people out of hospital. In 2001, there were 140,000 hospital admissions due to medication problems. And Ken and Julia believe these problems, to some extent, could have been picked up at the pharmacy level.

Through monitoring at Health Information Pharmacy, it has been shown that 1 in 6 prescriptions contain potential medication errors. Chemconsult™ picked up on them and in various cases actually kept people out of hospital. This does not only benefit the patient, but it's also a major benefit to society as a whole.

The Lee's have been able to take responsibility for their business and attack it head-on. This, they say, is one amazing result of Business Coaching.

The creation of a loyalty club is another system that was developed with the help of **ACTION**. The Platinum Care Club is the loyalty club exclusive to Health Information Pharmacy, and it offers members more than the normal loyalty club does. Members have access to a 24-hour, 7-day a week pharmacist hotline and a local area discount book, plus they have free access to a naturopath and a $10 gift voucher for every $150 spend. It is based on a referral system, which has been fantastic for building up the customer base. This fits in well with their core values, which are:

1. Reducing medication problems. This is done through Chemconsult™.

2. Empowerment of people. This is done through the incentive program and management development program in which people are empowered to step-up to the next level.

3. Strengthening their community. Unique marketing through Strategic Area Alliances and databases make this possible.

4. Helping the less fortunate. They donate $10 to the customer's favourite charity for every 3 people they refer to the loyalty club. Most business owners believe they should be donating to charity but don't have a vehicle through which to do so. This is a win-win situation that helps them grow their business while helping needy charities and people at the same time.

Health Information Pharmacy started testing and measuring everything they did. From this they stopped running newspaper ads that didn't work. They tested and measured headlines as well as guarantees. And while some of the guarantees got them into trouble with the Pharmacy Board, because the Pharmacy Act didn't allow them, Ken said this was a valuable lesson, as it put them right on track! It also helped them ascertain how far they could go in marketing, yet stay with their core values as well as the industry guidelines.

Pharmacists were also employed as managers. Systems and Key Performance Indicators were set up to track performances and Ken's routine changed dramatically. He went from working IN the business to working ON it, and now he is working on other people's businesses through franchising. He has also had the ability to create and be creative within the pharmacy setting.

The Coach's Story

Ken was one of the first potential coaching clients that actually interviewed ME. He had all these other business consultant and coaching company proposals laid out in front of him and he said, "Tell me why *ACTION* is different."

I saw something special in Ken; during the alignment consultation he shared his goals of wanting to make a difference in his profession and the community, of wanting to take these core values to help other pharmacists, not just locally, but globally, so I thought - this young man is special.

After 3 months Julia had started to leverage herself out of the business. After 6 months she was totally out. After 12 months Ken was also totally out although it took another 12 months to franchise the business.

The business outlook is great – the business sees itself as being very community-based and as a hub for community activities, especially in the health care arena. There is a naturopath in store. They also have strategic alliances with a chiropractor, massage therapist, gym, restaurant, real estate agent, financial planner and even holiday destinations.

The business culture is excellent. There is strong a culture within the business and externally as well. The pharmacy has been accepted quite well in the community, especially considering it was one of the first pharmacies to be accredited under quality care in Australia, with various press releases and articles being written about the work they are doing. In fact, through the work he has done with *ACTION*, Ken was nominated for *Young Australian of the Year 2000*.

The Outcome

"The pharmacy was making profit before we took over, but we have doubled the net profit in the last 3 years," says Ken. Turnover increased by 52% (from a large base), profit by 42% and average dollar sale from $30 to $46.

"And although there were not many targets in the early days, Health Information Pharmacy has now been vigorously setting them for the next 12 months. Ideally the target is domination in the marketplace. We have a strong financial position and a good aggressive group in terms of marketing and pharmaceutical care and how we position of ourselves in the market."

However, not everything has been a smooth run. There have been several challenges, which include a car going through the front window of the store one week before accreditation and a landlord who tried to close down the store. Then there were some challenges with the Pharmacy Board regarding some of their marketing strategies.

But the main challenge was discount pharmacies opening in the local area, and in some respects, this is what led Ken and Julia to choose the direction they did. Of course, like every other business, there were also staffing challenges that involved key team members leaving. The positive here is that other team members stepped up and accepted the challenge.

The end result has been massive. There is now a fully systemised business with over 100 systems. A 6-volume manual has been created that covers all areas of the business from finance to HR, and from dispensing to management and ownership. This has become a turnkey business for many pharmacists. The owners no longer work in-store, but still know what is happening.

A successful business model based on marketing, merchandising and team incentives has been developed. Health Information Pharmacy has shown that their systems and models can work in Castle Hill, and they are duplicating them throughout their franchise network.

Ken has taken an office in nearby Norwest Business Park, in Baulkham Hills, NSW and works purely on developing the franchise. However, he says this is just the beginning for Health Information Pharmacy, as they are now taking the business to the next level – from state to nationwide before going international.

Taking it to the next level is going to be traumatic, as Ken says he will be stepping out of his comfort zone of being a pharmacist once again to leading pharmacists, some of whom have a lot more experience in the industry than he does. "But I am looking forward to the challenge of making a difference in multiple areas," he says. "We will be sharing our values and beliefs throughout the pharmaceutical industry, and it's going to help patients."

And what of the future?

"It has been an exciting time with Greg Albert, my Business Coach. I'm looking forward to big things in the future. Greg is still involved as my coach, some 2 ?

years on, and he is also now the Business Development Manger at Health Information Pharmacy. One thing we have insisted on is that as each franchisee comes on board, they get a Business Coach for at least 3 months to ensure their success. I would recommend this as a must for any franchise out there. Working with **ACTION** has been incredible for the business. Every business owner should take it up because it is an investment in his or her own knowledge and skill development."

▌ Hairdresser's Turnover Doubles In 2 Months

Above all, we wish to avoid having a dissatisfied customer. We consider our customers a part of our organization, and we want them to feel free to make any criticism they see fit in regard to our merchandise or service. Sell practical, tested merchandise at reasonable profit, treat your customers like human beings — and they will always come back.

~ L.L. Bean ~

The Business

Name: Live It Up Hairdressing

Address: 149 Oak Road, Kirrawee, Sydney, NSW, 2232, Australia

Owners: Vance Fitzgerald and Renee Stuart

Type Of Business: Hairdresser

Business Sector: Service

Started: May 2001

Coach: Bernie Rorke

The Challenge

Hairdressing has got to be one of the most 'difficult' or fickle businesses around today. Let me explain what I mean. Generally speaking, youngsters who train as hairdressers do so because they either had no interest in anything else while at school or they didn't get high enough grades to pursue a different career path. They then learned all the stereotypes and prejudices about the business from other hairdressers during their apprenticeship. And being a technical business, their training focuses on the HOW of the business – how to cut hair, how to style it and how to colour it. The one thing they aren't taught is how to run a business.

Here's another difficulty they'll run into pretty soon – they'll need a shop front. You see, unlike other novices, hairdressers generally can't practice 'behind the scenes' until they've developed the necessary skills and confidence levels to 'go public' by opening a shop. Accountants can, lawyers can, and so can public relations consultants and electricians. But not hairdressers.

Of course, the young hairdresser can work for someone else, but I'm talking here about those who are a little more ambitious than that. I'm talking about those who want to run their own salon.

So, our aspiring business owner opens a salon and suddenly finds herself having to employ other people because she has rent to pay. Doing all the work herself usually won't cover the rent and other overheads. She also finds herself working long hours, often without being able to draw a wage. "I'll work hard for the first few years to get the business established," she tells herself, thinking it'll all pay off somewhere down the track. Trouble is, there are a few more surprises in store for her. You see, she'll find hairdressers come and go. And because they tend to build up an individual relationship with their clients, when they move on to work at another salon, so too do their clients. You'll have noticed how often salons run ads in the papers saying, 'We're pleased to announce that Julie now works here." This is a subtle way of 'stealing' the other salon's clients.

Our young business owner consequently finds herself slaving away IN the business herself instead of working ON it. She finds the latter impossible to do because it's such a technical business and besides, it's what she's been trained at. Her mentors and teachers all did the same thing and have reinforced this perception during her apprenticeship.

So she burns out, decides to sell and is surprised to discover she gets offered nothing for the business. Not an ideal situation, is it? No wonder she bails out with a terrible impression of what being in business is all about?

Now I know this may be a stereotypical situation, but it needn't be. Here's a great example.

Vance's Story

We are a young, soon-to-be-married couple who had very little knowledge about running a business when we opened our hairdressing salon back in May, 2001. And like most in that situation, all we really had going for us at the time was loads of enthusiasm. We were eager to give it a go, work hard and do whatever it took to succeed.

And, so far so good. Or should I say, so far so typical. We found the going tough.

Our business was going very slowly, and we were doing all the work, yet there was no profit.

The business settled down with, on average, 240 customers bringing in $2,300 a week. To make matters worse, when another hairdresser opened up only 20m down the road, needless to say, we were more than a little unsure about our future.

The Moment Of Truth

Fortunately, we were willing to do anything to ensure the business' success, so I went and got work as a builder's labourer to bring in much needed cashflow. I also attended one of Brad Sugars' seminars.

It was there that I realised the importance of getting professional help, and filled in a form to make contact with one of Brad's coaches.

We wanted the business to improve. You see, while sales were running at $2,300 a week, we had very little in the way of consistent marketing strategies, our team communication was very low and there were no key performance indicators. But we did have some goals, which were to:

- Increase sales from approximately $2,300 to $3,000 a week within 6 months.

- Set up a good business structure or system.

- Increase marketing strategies.

- Obtain a better understanding of business.

- Enable me to quit my outside job.

- Purchase another hairdressing business.

All the ingredients were in place to begin working ON the business in earnest. We had come to the realisation that things just had to improve. We also were able to recognise our shortcomings.

We lacked motivation and vision at times. This, I know, is a common problem faced by many in business today. We also weren't accountable to anyone. Again, a common problem. You see, because you're running your own show usually means you don't have anyone to answer to, except yourself. Now many, shall I say, less experienced business owners will know that this isn't an advantage at all – it can be a huge disadvantage. This is where the Business Coach comes in. In our case, we hired Bernie Rorke.

The Coach's Story

I started by concentrating firstly on sales, which had to be increased dramatically as profit was minimal.

We introduced testing and measuring strategies to find out where the customers were coming from, and we surveyed every customer. At the bottom of the survey page we ran a referral promotion, and obtained an average of just under one referral per existing client. The referral was contacted and booked in for a half price haircut. This bought a number of new clients in to the business quite quickly.

It's funny how many business owners instinctively want to cut prices to increase profit. This is something I never advocate.

Pricing was increased by 10% and a new focus on average dollar sale was introduced. We then concentrated on developing systems within the business. We broke the whole procedure into stages, ranging from the initial customer phoning in, making the booking, and greeting them on arrival. We reviewed each stage and made sure we were giving the client the best possible experience.

If we were going to generate a flow of new clients into the business, we needed to exceed their expectations during their visit to ensure they come back and, hopefully, have them refer others to us as well.

We started giving 'thank you' and 'welcome' cards to new clients and referrals, and we reviewed critical non-essentials. We began to create as many magical moments for the customer as possible, to get them talking about 'Live It Up'. And it certainly paid off.

The Outcome

The business doubled in turnover from $2,300 a week to over $4,000 a week within 2 months. That's nearly a 100% increase.

Profit has also increased dramatically, enabling the owners to implement some improvements to their business, such as installing a computerised counter system and a new counter. Team communication has also increased dramatically, and team morale is very high.

Renee and Vance are now able to afford a reasonable honeymoon and are able to relax knowing the business will run on its own in their absence. A very nice outcome indeed. But don't just take my word for it. Vance and Renee say they've gained both personally and professionally from the experience.

"Turnover has increased, which has given us the money and opportunity to build the business the way we desire," says Vance. "We've gained experience with ideas, and bought books and tapes to help snowball the business. We can now also pay for our wedding and honeymoon. We've also got someone to be accountable to, we have been taught the importance of the team to the business, and we have attended seminars, which has given the coaching program even greater value."

Vance says they have gained much on a personal level as well. "We are now less anxious, we feel more like leaders and have realised the importance of balancing our relationships with the business."

▌ Builder Renovates His Business And Cements A Great Future

Concentrate your strengths against your competitor's relative weaknesses.

~ *Bruce Henderson* ~

The Business

Name: Beautiful Bathrooms Of Sydney

Address: Golf Avenue, Mona Vale, Sydney, NSW, 2103, Australia

Owner: Shane Besson

Type Of Business: Bathroom Renovation

Business Sector: Building

Started: August 2001

Coach: Patrick Bright

The Challenge

Shane Besson lives in the Northern Beaches region of the Sydney metropolitan area, 40 minutes north of the Sydney CBD. And because he is in the business of renovating bathrooms, his business has no fixed address. He has no shop front, rather he likes to concentrate his efforts on the large business zone of the Sydney CBD and Northern Suburbs.

His client base consists mostly of homeowners and investors. With this comes every type of person from the young first home buyers to business people with particular requirements, right through to retirees who appreciate a person who is pleasant to deal with. As you can imagine, all these different groups have differing requirements, which makes operating successfully in this business, a major challenge.

Time is a big issue for most people these days. There is never enough time and everyone seems constantly busy. Recognising this turned out to be one of Shane's major advantages as far as his business was concerned – it gave him the opportunity to excel by taking up as little of it as possible by being swift and impressive with construction. It's also important to strike the right balance with your communication efforts too, as most people don't want too much or too little of it from you. Shane says that he finds people in his community to be extremely busy – and they like to feel important. "You may laugh at how simple this is," he says. "The next time you deal with any business, remember how important you felt with them."

So how has he coped? How has this typical builder-turned-businessman managed to survive in today's fast-paced high-tech world? How has this tradesman managed to adapt to the rigours of the business world? This is his story.

Shane's Story

I have been in the Building Industry for 15 years now, but I like to say I've only been in the Business Industry for 18 months. I believe our market will continue growing rapidly as the population grows. The need for homes is growing, but there is not enough room. Existing homes are ageing rapidly, as well as increasing in value and this, in turn, is resulting in an increase in demand for renovation work.

A big advantage for my business is that it is widely accepted in the community that tradespeople are generally slack with communication, slack in appearance, and slack in attitude. It is widely accepted that the trades, in comparison to other industries, are unprofessional and that good tradespersons are very rare. Just ask anyone if they have had a bad experience with a tradesperson.

I see this as an opportunity. If you can exceed expectations and do the job sooner than they expect, you'll get great referrals from customers in what is generally a referral-based business. This alone has contributed substantially to the growth of Beautiful Bathrooms Of Sydney.

My biggest challenge was, and still is, finding and training like-minded and motivated people. Like many industries, this is the greatest challenge, especially if you have a huge desire to grow. How much growth? Our primary aim is to be the industry leader in Sydney, then Brisbane, Melbourne and Auckland through phenomenal service and a referral-based business.

So how did I get there? From being a one man show!

When I first started out on my own, I was a sole contractor and spent most of my time working for someone else. What little time I had left, I spent trying to build up my own clients. I mostly contracted to large building firms and found dissatisfaction in them reaping the rewards from all my hard work, with little benefit in return. This pattern went on for several years. I knew there was a path to success and financial independence, but I was not on it.

Before I started this business, my financial situation was dismal. And so was my commitment to that side of my business. I lacked direction, I would go from one job to the next and I had no plan. I was in debt when I started, and I had to pay for coaching with my credit card. Yet I just knew I had to make some changes, as what I was doing on my own was not getting me where I wanted to go.

The Moment Of Truth

In a good month I would gross between $4,000 to $5,000. And I wanted to make $10,000 a month and more, but didn't know how. After years of moving between working for customers and other builders (and some travelling overseas – something someone might normally do in their mid twenties) I became hugely frustrated with both my financial situation and myself. I absolutely knew that I had the brains, and the ability, to achieve more than this (as I had with sport through my teens and early twenties). It was this raw dissatisfaction that drove me to finding out where I was going wrong and to do something about it.

I decided to take responsibility for my own situation, as no one else created the mess I was in or my feeling of dissatisfaction. I could simply not believe I was 29 and had less in the bank than when I was 23.

It actually began to depress me as well as frustrate me. It was at that point, in April 2001, that I made a decision to change and get some business help.

Having made the decision to learn how to build, own and operate a successful business, I began to attend to a lot of seminars and signed on to many business development programs. Patrick Bright was a guest speaker at one of these seminars, and he spoke of a business coaching success story that just happened to be in the same industry as the one I wanted to create my business in. It just clicked. I realised that what I needed to do was enlist Patrick's help.

Basically, Pat had to start from scratch with me. I only used a few business principles at that time, and mostly thought about what I was producing and not about the business side of things. So the challenge for me was to truly start thinking like a businessperson and not as a builder. I found this very hard indeed after 15 years on the tools.

Pat began by suggesting I read specific books to educate myself as much as possible. This, he said, would get me up to speed with the business tools I would need to get started on the right path. He also suggested I set some simple and effective weekly goals to get things moving quickly. Create some scripts, get new business cards, put my prices up, create a more efficient quoting system, charge for design proposals, place some ads in the local paper to generate leads, and work on my referral strategies.

We developed a Plan Of Action. This included starting weekly coaching sessions and getting real about my goals, which I set as follows: to go from being a contractor turning over $40,000 to $60,000 per year to a Business Owner with a company turning over $1.8 million per year in 3 years.

I needed to have a grasp of the business language and principals, and I had to learn quickly. I wanted to get started right there and then. I was eager to get going as I had discovered there was a way to grow my business. Luckily I didn't, and I now see why Pat held me back from diving straight in as long as he could. By setting goals of books to read, tapes to listen to and things to achieve was just excellent. The 2-day business workshop I attended was so good I did it twice during my 12-month coaching program – I got more out of it the second time. You don't often invest 2 days straight working on your business, and it was the best thing I could have done.

Introducing changes to the business and my routine was the single biggest challenge I faced, even though I wanted to be successful and to achieve my goals.

The discipline and effort I needed in comparison to how I was doing things previously was a massive challenge in the beginning. I did not adjust well to it and it took time. Even though I wanted the outcome, the reality of the work I had to do to achieve it was overwhelming at times to say the least. Pat could have sacked me a dozen times for disagreements and not getting done what was needed, but he didn't. It took me a long time to realise how being slow to implement change was killing my new business.

After missing a few of my targets and being very disappointed, I began to truly see that, as well as making changes in the business, I had to change myself if I wanted to reach my goals. It was only after seeing my failures and truly understanding why they occurred, that I committed more time to my business and changed my routine to suit the business more than myself.

So when it came time to do some Testing and Measuring, I realised we didn't have any real benchmarks to work off. But we started with lead generation and conversion, and continued from there. And wow, from someone who thought they got just about every contract they tendered for, the raw percentages were a real eye opener. Pat simply smiled, as he knew we had plenty of room for improvement.

The Coach's Story

I met Shane at a business seminar where I was a guest speaker. He was a bit concerned at how he was going to pay for the coaching as he was in debt but he needed help. I gave him Brad Sugars' tape called *3 Steps To Profitable Marketing* and performed a diagnostic consultation to assess his business. I showed him how he couldn't afford NOT to take on a coach based on what he wanted to achieve and what he had achieved so far. He agreed and I carried out an Alignment Consultation.

The outcome of this led me to recommend he project a highly professional image. He needed to learn scripts, start Testing and Measuring, and thinking about better time and self-management strategies. I also wanted him to begin building strategic alliances with suppliers to get deals.

He thought his conversion rate (from prospects to clients) was 70%, but we tested it and found it to be around 30%. Shane needed to change his beliefs about sales and get more confidence. He also needed to put in place some guarantees, do a Cashflow analysis and increase his networking.

This certainly presented him with some challenges, especially concerning his beliefs about selling, business, customers and money. Getting him off the tools and onto the business was another major challenge, and one I decided to work gently on. Like getting him to finish goals before he started new ones, and to use scripts consistently. I needed him to sacrifice some recreation time to focus on achieving his goals.

I overcame these challenges by being persistent. I wouldn't let him off the hook, even though at times it felt like we were treading water with the growth of the business. I have learnt that if you let your clients go forward too quickly, nothing gets done properly and you end up with a bigger problem than you had before you started.

So, how did I get his business moving in the right direction? I got him to go to networking breakfasts. These produced one of his largest sources of new business for the first 6 months. I then got him to call-up past clients to ask for testimonials and referrals.

The Outcome

The first 6 months were frustrating. Shane says Pat knew he was beginning to understand what it took to be a successful businessperson, but it was not until the second 6-month period of his 12-month program that it all came together. "I truly exercised massive discipline as well as made some very tough decisions that turned things around," explains Pat.

Shane says some walls are harder for some people to brake through than others. "But when you get there, it can be one of the most amazing experiences of you life. I am not the same person I was 12 months ago. I truly have to thank Pat for his patience and perseverance. For the 2001/2002 financial year, I recorded over 3 times the turnover of my previous best year – that's a 300% increase in 12 months, and we are on target to double that again for the 2002/2003 financial year.

Shane now has a profitable business with a team of 3 employees and around 30 contractors on the books. He now only provides quotes and organizes the work – he doesn't work with tools himself anymore. He is making 3 to 5 times more per month than he was 12 months ago, and he's not working as hard for it - physically or mentally. He made enough money to purchase an investment property with his father and to start renovating it, and plans to sell it when it's completed, and to buy, and renovate, more. He's certainly come a long way.

▌ Gym Instructor Builds A Healthy Business

In business for yourself, not by yourself.

~ Ray Kroc ~

The Business

Name: Fitness Shortly (now Ignite Health Pty Ltd)

Address: 276 Devonshire Street, Surrey Hills, NSW, 2010, Australia

Owner: Jamie Short

Type Of Business: Gym and Personal Training Studio

Business Sector: Health & Fitness

Started: 1999

Coach: Patrick Bright

The Challenge

Being self-employed has a certain ring to it that many find appealing. But running your own show is not a bed of roses. A self-employed person normally starts out with just one employee; themself. And that suits them fine; no one else to worry about, and none of those other people who make all the mistakes, it's just them.

The self-employed person usually trusts no one other than themself to get the job done. They'll say things like: "I am my business." Or, in their sales pitch: "You'll be dealing directly with me and I'm the owner of the business." Or, "If you want something done right, you've got to do it yourself." Or, "Everything is under my control so I know that it's done right."

Being self-employed is usually the first jump on the entrepreneurial ladder and for most, it's the only jump. In fact, most entrepreneurs never seem to get past this level of growth in their business.

The truth is you really can't call it a business; you've really got to call it a JOB. And of course, you do know what J-O-B stands for, don't you? Just Over Broke.

What's more, this job is most probably one of the worst jobs in the world. I think it's put best by this quote, taken from one of my live seminars: "Most people thought they worked for an idiot BEFORE they started their own business."

I really don't think most people who start their own business know what they're getting themselves into. In fact, most look at it as something glamorous, exciting, and with such a sense of newfound freedom that they're fooled into believing wealth is just a few days, weeks or months away.

The Self-Employed are trapped by the limited 'doing' vision that is a part of being an employee. As an example, computer technicians who start their own businesses usually see themselves servicing people's computers and would be extremely happy if they could get enough business to keep themselves, and only themselves, extremely busy.

This results in your business life feeling just like a see-saw. You'll spend half your life chasing the work, or doing Marketing, Sales and Administration. Then you'll have so much work to do you'll have to flip over and start doing the work…

Doing the Work is one side of the see-saw, and Sales and Marketing is the other.

Chase the work, do the work, chase the work, do the work, chase the work, do the work … and so on …

It's this see-saw that stops a Self-Employed Entrepreneur from ever really getting ahead. It's also this see-saw that gets Self-Employed people to make one of two decisions: either they give it up and go back and get a job, or they take the plunge and jump in at the deep end of business and make the decision to grow their business by moving up the ladder.

This is what Jamie Short did. This is what he has to say.

Jamie's Story

I was pretty much a one-man band. I had one guy doing some personal training sessions for me, and that guy was me! I was the technician, manager, owner and entrepreneur all at the same time. The different hats that I was wearing could have filled an entire hat store.

So, what exactly do I do, you may ask? Well, if you ever get up really early, around 5 or 6am, you might see those crazy people running up and down the beach or in the park. Yes, that's me, encouraging people to get into shape at weird and ungodly times of the day.

I spent the other half of my day running around Sydney training clients at their homes, their offices or at a couple of different gyms. I didn't have many systems in place at all, and the reality was it was going to be a miracle if I could achieve my goal of owning my own gym in the next 12 months.

The Moment Of Truth

I was busy and earned a good little package, but I knew there was more. I was doing all my 30 or 40 sessions per week, trying to do the marketing, finances, admin and everything else. I was wearing all the hats and not enjoying it at all. I had enough pain. It was time to call for some help.

I have always known what Pat Bright did for a living, but I was scared to take the plunge and to take on his services. Yes, there was a lot of fear that came up. Issues like, can I afford it? And the fear of failure and thoughts of what other people where going to say. Then I attended one of Pat's sales training courses. He mentioned a few keynotes, like playing above the line and taking responsibility for my actions and having ownership. This really struck some emotions; I had certainly had enough pain running my own business.

So after finally making the call, Pat and I got under way. The Alignment Report was first, and as the saying goes, you don't know what you don't know. Well, I certainly didn't know what had to be done to run a successful business. Pat and I put together an **ACTION** plan and away we went.

The first thing we did was to increase prices (wow, what a head shift that was). I quickly became one of the most expensive personal trainers in Sydney and was defiantly the most expensive in the main gym were I was training. People certainly took notice of that. Other aspects of the plan involved filling in quiet parts of the day, such as   the down times during lunch time and in the early afternoon with special training sessions. Forming strong strategic alliances proved to be very successful within the first 3 to 4 months.

I had increased my turnover by 20% in a couple of months and was testing and measuring all inquiries. This provided me with very valuable information down the track.

I then began to realise the importance of working ON the business instead of IN it. I began training up another trainer and getting him to do some of my sessions as well as more work. This freed me up to do some marketing.

As the months passed, I found myself getting busier and busier. I had formed some strong strategic alliances and was receiving great referrals from them. Systems were in place and they were working very well. Referrals from existing clients were coming in, as we did a promotion involving massages for those who referred on clients who signed up for a set amount of sessions. This was so successful that I had to slow down the marketing campaign – I had become busier than I could cope with.

However, the real challenge began with the next step – acquiring a studio.

Ever since I was 14-years old I had a dream of owning my own gym – a place where people would come to train, have fun, and enjoy hanging out at. Well this dream came true.

I teamed up with an old friend whom I went through university with and played rugby against. We decided to tackle the gym together. We merged our businesses and formed Ignite Health Pty Ltd. We were then on the hunt … with Pat being the General back at the Officer's Mess, and us being the front line soldiers being sent out toreceive all the hits and war wounds while searching for, and finding, a business and business premises.

We wanted to start up our own gym from scratch, but Pat convinced us to find an existing one that was doing poorly – one whose owner's wanted to sell for a reason – as this way we'd get a better deal than having to wear the set-up costs of a new one.

Every Saturday we'd read the Business For Sale section of the paper as well as Business for Sale Magazines. We looked at dozens over the next few months, putting in offers that were all rejected. Then one day we finally came across a hot one. The ad read, 'Gym for Sale. Require urgent sale for personal reasons. Great price.'

Well, after looking at the business and using Pat's business buying checklist, this looked too good to be true.

After 8 weeks of negotiations and going back and forth from the solicitors, accountants, financial lenders, and of course Pat, we struck a deal.

This is how it worked: The original asking price for the business was $160,000. Equipment was insured for just over $100,000 and would sell second-hand for around $80,000 as most of it was only 18-months old. They wanted $50,000 for the goodwill/income it was producing. The business had been going for 6 years, however, it showed little profit – the systems were in a mess. The owners were a husband and wife team and she was pregnant with their 3rd child. Furthermore, she was ready to give birth in the next few weeks – now that's real urgency to sell. Initially my business partner and I were prepared to pay up to $120,000 for the business, as we loved it, its location, and its potential. However, Pat wouldn't let us do that and he kept saying we needed to get a better deal. It was as if it was his money that was on the line.

Pat asked what our absolute dream price to pick this business up at would be. He wanted to know the dream price at which we could sell it for a profit the next day without doing anything to it. I replied $70,000, so Pat asked how good would it be if we could get it for $60,000?

I got very excited and asked how could we possibly do that, as the owners had already knocked back offers in excess of $100,000. Pat said those buyers had now gone, and the owners wanted to sell urgently, so all we had to do was to find out what, other than money, they wanted, and then give it to them, provided we got the business for a great price.

We came up with a strategy – saying this was the best offer they were going to get and we were their only option to take over the lease. The final price was agreed on at $60 000, with a clause that we had 30 days from the agreement date to walk away before exchanging contracts.

The learning curve that Darren (my business partner) and I went through was absolutely incredible. I have learnt more in the past 3 to 6 months than I did over the past 5 years of operating my own personal training business.

The gym now consists of 350m2 of equipment on one whole floor. We offer a unique service where we guarantee that one of our expert trainers will look after four members at once, each having their own program depending on their goals and needs. This is a guaranteed personalised service. We also offer yoga groups, boxing groups, massage, as well as a solarium. We have nine trainers, hundreds of members and made a profit within the first 2 months of operation. When I first started with Pat, the business had a turnover of about $35,000 a year – we now do that in a month.

Our new vision is to have four of these gyms around Sydney within the next 3 or 4 years. And by that I mean we actually buy the property first, and then establish the gym at the premises.

The Coach's Story

I met Jamie through a referral of a mutual friend, to help him with his business, before I became an **ACTION** Coach. After I became an **ACTION** Coach, I went back through all my old contacts and appointments to see if any of them were ready to get serious about their business. He was a very concerned at how he was going to pay for coaching as he was only turning over $35,000 a year. I wouldn't normally take on a client with such a low turnover, however, there was something about him that told me this guy was coachable and would do whatever it took to achieve his goals. So the following week I did the Alignment Consultation.

Jamie was so full of passion and energy, however, he lacked the direction and focus to keep him on track to achieve his goals.

He needed to free himself of the $20 per hour jobs he was doing. Initially he had to do more personal training sessions with his free time to increase his cashflow. And he needed a more professional image to go with his profile. The price rise we were going to put in place would make him the most expensive trainer around.

We introduced scripts and developed a referral program, which worked outstandingly well. We started to test and measure everything, and concentrated on improving his time management/self-management skills. We built strategic alliances with other health professionals as a way of generating new leads, as Jamie didn't have the cashflow to invest in marketing. His conversion rate also needed some work.

As a way of increasing cashflow, we put in place some guarantees, and produced 10 paid-in-advance training session packs (at a reduced rate) to increase client's training sessions per week. This worked very well. We discovered from our testing and measuring that the business was 90% referral. This convinced us to develop more strategies aimed at increasing the flow of referrals to the business. We produced an e-mail newsletter, and tried several different types of flyers, which didn't work so we dropped them and went back to what was working – referrals and strategic alliances.

We certainly faced some interesting challenges along the way. Jamie's time was limited, as he was already working over 70 hours per week, so we had to free him up from the non-income producing stuff. This was not easy, as he didn't have anyone to delegate to.

We introduced systems to his business and got him to use scripts consistently. Keeping him focused on his weekly goals without letting himself set another dozen each week was also a major challenge. So was trying to get some balance back into his life.

Jamie was a goal-setting machine. Some days I felt lazy after finding out what he had achieved each week and comparing it to my list of things achieved. He would always take on more than he could chew. However 80% of the time he would knock off the goals we'd set together.

Jamie's passion and focus due to the clarity of his goals, I think, was the main driving factor for him. Coaching him was like having a tiger by the tail most of the time.

Sometimes I came up with novel solutions to his challenges. I got him to start to document what he was doing with his clients and to build a training manual so he could train another trainer without it taking up too much of his time. We then set about recruiting a new team member. He also contacted his clients and asking for testimonials and referrals.

In addition to all this, Jamie also attended the two-day workshop and got a ton of information and more motivation from it.

The Outcome

Jamie Short is a changed man. And so is his business and financial outlook. He has achieved an enormous amount in such a short time. If you were to ask him what were the main benefits he received from having a Business Coach, this is what he'd say. Take a look at it closely:

- Increased my turnover by 500% in twelve months.

- Increased my team from being a one-man band to managing 15 people.

- Saved over $100,000 in purchasing a business.

- Went from no strategic alliances to having over 6 that actively refer clients.

- Being able to systemise my business.

- 90% success rate with my marketing campaigns (and being able to measure the success as well).

- Increased my client base 650% in twelve months.

That's not bad in anybody's language. He now has a profitable business that works without him. He has a gym, which was his dream goal, and has a team so he doesn't have to do all the work himself. In fact, he can now even have a holiday for a couple of weeks each year, if he wants to. And he is turning over more per month than he was per year when he first got serious about his business.

But don't take my word for it. Here's more of what he has to say.

"Looking back over the year, I can say that it wasn't all smooth sailing, and there were some long hours doing homework (that I set for myself). Pat always loves to test the boundaries and find the limits (that's why we get on … I think), but it was oh so rewarding.

"To see what has been accomplished and to have the future mapped out is so inspiring and fulfilling. Over the past 12 months, we have achieved an incredible amount of work. I have brought a gym with my new business partner and saved over $100,000 on the purchase price. Our services have expanded and we now offer the following:

- Personal training (one-on-one or groups).

- Massage (work or at home).

- Corporate health services (team building, massage, health seminars, exercise groups).

- Success coaching.

- Packaged meals.

- Nutritional analysis.

- Yoga and boxing classes.

- Health and fitness assessments.

- Personalised exercise programs.

"I could be here all day going on about how much my life and business has changed, but until you experience it yourself, you will never know the real benefits of having a coach."

▌ Café Owners Make Spare Time For Themselves – And More Money

---

Entrepreneurs are simply those who understand that there is little difference between obstacle and opportunity and are able to turn both to their advantage.

~ Victor Kiam ~

The Business

Name: Café Istanbul

Address: 156 Cuba Street, Wellington, New Zealand

Owners: Wendy East and Cengiz Altinkaya

Type Of Business: Restaurant

Business Sector: Food & Beverage/Service

Started: 1991

Coach: Steve McDonald

The Challenge

The restaurant business has its own unique set of challenges like unsocial working hours, long working days (and nights) and a high turnover of staff. Behind the scenes in the kitchen, there are challenges too concerning stocking levels, choice of menus, preparation time and the minimisation of wastage. The usual result is that restaurant owners don't lead a normal life, resulting all too often in them eventually selling up or burning out.

Fortunately for the owners of Café Istanbul, they decided to take action to ensure this didn't happen to them. And it so easily could have. You see, their business was stable but unspectacular. Sales were declining, and there were continual challenges recruiting and retaining a competent team. They were getting good numbers of diners in on Thursdays, Fridays and Saturdays, but for the remainder of the week, they were operating marginally at best, or at a slight loss.

The owners were working 7 nights a week, covering every role in the business. They hadn't had a real break in 9 years. And things didn't look like changing – if they didn't start doing something differently, they'd be trapped forever, until they either burned out, or walked out.

Wendy's Story

Our business is Café Istanbul. It's a Turkish restaurant in Wellington City. It's a family-owned business that we've run for 11 years now. I look after the front of house, manage the staff and see to sales.

Over the last 6 months to a year, we've noticed a big growth in the upper end of Cuba St, where we are situated. There's a lot more people – a lot more foot traffic – and many bars and cafes are being developed in the street. There are also a lot of inner city apartments in our area now.

While many of our customers are students, we also cater for those between the ages of 25 and 45; we have quite a few 40th birthday parties here. We also get 21sts and even 60th and 70th birthday parties, so our customer base is quite vast.

Our Café is very well known. Everyone in the area knows who we are and where we are. Those who haven't been to us before will always ring up to find out. We have a lot of regular customers.

We obviously want to pitch to the people with the most money, so we're thinking of aiming at city dwellers, the apartment people, in the next marketing campaign. These tend to be aged 25 to 35 or 40, have a good disposable income and probably no children or dependants. They have that extra money to spend on going out.

We're definitely considering opening up for lunch. We have done that once before and there just wasn't enough foot traffic. But we've noticed in recent times that on a Thursday, Friday and Saturday (and even Sunday) there are a lot of people about and they're all looking for somewhere to have lunch.

We faced several challenges before we met Steve, particularly regarding staffing in the kitchen (we used to import chefs from Turkey), team building with our front of house team and getting the right people. Other challenges included putting systems in place that, perhaps, we hadn't thought of before.

Finding the right staff had always been a big problem ... we'd advertise and basically end up just having to take the first available person rather than the right person. Steve has given me some really good information and guidelines on how to choose the right person rather than be hasty and choose the wrong person, because when running a restaurant, you need people; people on the floor and not just people who are available to work.

In the past, we were basically happy with what we made from the business. Even though we could probably have made a lot more, we didn't try. And with putting different systems in place, like managing our booking times and getting more 'bums on seats', we've been able to increase the number of people we serve, and of course, the number of dollars we take. So there's definitely been a really good increase since we've started working with Steve.

The Moment of Truth

We did think about coaching late last year, but it wasn't until we received a letter from Steve, out of the blue, that we actually thought about it more seriously and Cengiz and I decided to go ahead with it. It just came at the right time and also he made a lot of good points in the letter, which caught Cengiz' eye; you know, made him think, "Maybe this guy can help us."

Steve helped us trouble shoot areas and come up with solutions we perhaps wouldn't have thought of. We've got a really good booking management system now, and we've diverted the phone so we take all of the bookings, which we can now manage better. Before it was left up to the kitchen staff, many of whom could hardly speak English. It was a case of when it was full, it was full. We also introduced a system to use on the night to allocate tables and direct people to them. We now know who's going where and how long they need at their table. So it's little things like this that have been put together to make the whole running of the restaurant a lot smoother.

There were certainly challenges that we had to overcome along the way. Most things went together quite well, though. I know Cengiz had systems to put in place in the kitchen, and he really had to push his team to do them, because it was something different and they perhaps weren't used to it. In terms of the front of house team, definitely trying to get them to learn how to sell and how to up-sell was a challenge, as some of our team weren't confident in this area.

What have we achieved so far? I'd say there's probably been a 15-20% increase in the number of customers we get.

We've also found someone to look after the restaurant on different nights when we're not there. So we've been able to take more time off. Previously we were working 6 out of 7 nights, and as we took alternate nights off, Cengiz and I would hardly ever see each other! So coaching has made it a lot easier … back then we weren't taking any time off, maybe one night each, but now I've got 2 or 3 and Cengiz has 4 nights off. So we're a lot better off. In the past I would never have been able to sit here, work on systems and put different things together, whereas before, when I really had to, I didn't have the time to spare.

We are currently training a new team member to become involved in managing the business so our next challenge is to put systems in place so that he can do it. That's one of the things I have put together; a procedure manual and a team training manual. Our aim is to go overseas next year, so we need to have everything in place so we can actually take the time off.

The Coach's Story

My suggestions included the following:

- Increase prices.

- Train the team to up-sell off the menu.

- Train the team to serve the customer consistently and well.

- Sack the staff that didn't perform and set up a team of great performers.

- Stop recruitment ads that didn't work and advertise for the people they wanted, not the skills they needed.

Our plan of action also included systemising the kitchen ordering, as well as the day-to-day routines. It was important to make it possible for anyone to open up, shut down, stock the bar, and order kitchen supplies, etc. We also needed to create cleaning, ordering and maintenance systems, and this work needed to be delegated to team members.

Next we needed to select and groom a manager who could operate the restaurant without the owners needing to be present. Systems were set up to enable this to happen, checklists were then created, as well as a requirements manual and rosters, to ensure that routine tasks were systemized and the system followed.

We then set about identifying our target market. Once this was done, we concentrated on designing our marketing to appeal to those targets. We started collecting customer details and created a database that we could market to. We raised the bar on customer service and established the expectation of excellent service, and actively managed team membership around this expectation.

Everything was measured. The aim was to know the numbers every week – and by this I mean the number of tables, the number of diners, and average dollar sale. Every opportunity was taken to look for additional sales opportunities.

Testing and measuring played a vital role in transforming this business. All marketing efforts were tested and measured, and all procedures that didn't work were stopped. All marketing is now tested on a small scale before it gets expensive. All business Key Performance Indicators – sales, average sale, number of diners, stock rollover and wastage, portion measuring – they are all measured and monitored.

Since coaching began, sales are up 20% and customer numbers and the average dollar sale are consistently up on a weekly basis.

The team is now more stable, and more productive. They have a greater focus on creating an exceptional dining experience for every customer, every time.

The owners now work 4 or 5 days per week only, and have time off together every week. They now have a life. And they are well on the way to having a manager who can run the business without them, for longer periods. The team is far more productive, happier and stable. We are still improving the team every month, and we have a recruiting system that consistently delivers excellent prospects for them.

The kitchen is now essentially a self-sustaining, self-contained unit. Orders, cleaning and kitchen activities are self-managed by the kitchen team. The owners don't need to continually supervise that area any longer.

The routine of ordering, daily team management, maintenance, and daily operations are almost at a point where the systems run the business.

The Outcome

Wendy and Cengiz are working towards having all these systems and the right people in place so they can concentrate on establishing a tourist business overseas. They're planning on spending at least 3 months away from the business soon, checking out various options. Longer term, they're either thinking of selling the restaurant or leasing it and settling overseas.

They say the best thing about working with a coach has been the accountability that makes sure they do the work. "This would never have got done, I don't think, if Steve hadn't made us set goals and tasks, and actually achieve them," Wendy said. "It's got us into good habits whereas before, trying to get something done was a mammoth task, even if it was a little thing. So definitely, setting the goals and tasks and achieving them has been our biggest achievement."

Wendy recommends every business owner should consider a Business Coach. "I would definitely recommend it. He has such a wealth of knowledge. And for someone like myself who hasn't had a lot to do with running a business before, I've learnt quite a lot from him and have certainly benefited from it."

▌Software Consultant Now Has The Customers She Deserves

I don't want to do business with those who don't make a profit, because they can't give the best service.

~ Lee Bristol ~

The Business

Name: Achieve! Ltd

Address: 1 Seddon Street, Upper Hutt, New Zealand

Owner: Mary Sue Severn

Type Of Business: Computer software sales, implementation and training

Business Sector: Information Technology

Started: 1999

Coach: Steve McDonald

The Challenge

Working on your own can be one of the most difficult, and demanding, things you can do. It can also be soul destroying if you're not careful. Isolation, lack of stimulation and the real possibility of loosing your bearings, both mentally and professionally, are all very real challenges that today's sole operator faces.

Many thrive under these conditions, but the vast majority don't. They may eek out a meagre existence for a while, but the truth of the matter is, it's a tough environment in which to thrive.

The smart operators recognise the signals when they're beginning to approach dangerous territory and take action. Take Mary Sue Severn, for instance. She's an Act! certified consultant. Act! is a contact management software package, which has over 70% market share in the world, and is used by more than 4 million people.

It helps people manage their communications with their staff, co-workers, customers and suppliers.

While Mary Sue is based in Upper Hutt, she serves all of New Zealand. Most of her customer base is centred between Palmerston North and Christchurch, but she has customers up and down the country. And they come from all walks of life.

"There's no business, I would say, that Act! doesn't work for," she says. "We have travel companies, recruitment companies, financial advisers ... I've got utilities, wholesalers ... I've got retailers. You name it, anybody can use Act!"

OK, so how can a coach help someone like Mary Sue? What, apart from the obvious, can be achieved by having a coach in a situation like this?

Mary Sue's Story

Act! is not marketed really strongly in the Asia/Pacific region, and particularly not in New Zealand. It's not like, you know, there's a massive advertising campaign for Act!, so most sales, I think, have come through word of mouth.

I've been a user of Act! for 15 years now, since its DOS days. But I've been an Act! certified consultant for 3 years. The sorts of people who use this product are ... people ... small to medium-sized businesses with 3 to 20 users would be typical. They have a need to communicate regularly with their customers and would want to collect information about them beyond just their names and addresses.

When I say the product hasn't been marketed, I mean as a brand. The owners (of Act!) do some advertising throughout the Asia/Pacific region, but it's not heavily advertised. You'd never see it on TV, for example. So from a brand point-of-view it's not heavily marketed.

From a personal point-of-view, looking at Achieve! Ltd, my reputation is continually growing through word-of-mouth and through some of the advertising that I do.

Before I met Steve, I certainly faced challenges such as IT issues, and accepting my own worth – and coming from a user-angle as opposed to an IT-angle, which is where a lot of Act! consultants come into the game. They tend to know everything about computers, but they don't know much about people, customers, and business processes, and can answer any technical question that's fired at them but I was the exact opposite. You know, you could throw me with a simple tech question, but man, I could tell you anything about how to market it, or how to improve communication within the office. I could certainly do that part of it. I had a real hard time expecting payment for some of those technical services I provided.

The Moment Of Truth

Well, it's quite funny really, because it all began when my husband and I met Steve McDonald and his wife at a bed and breakfast over in the Wairarapa, and we just got talking. I thought, "Oh, I like this guy." And then about a month later we got in touch again. I called him and we just worked it out from there. I had used a business mentoring service in the past, but I found I wasn't getting out of it what I needed to. I think it was structured differently from the way Steve works.

Steve helped me understand that I was providing value to my customers, especially over time, as I've learned more and more, and now it's pretty hard to stump me in IT areas. I needed to really get over that emotional hurdle; that what I did was actually of value to my customers. And I needed to start charging for things I was previously giving away. Steve said he actually bumped into a customer of mine who said I provided an amazing service, but never bothered sending an invoice. Well, that said it all to me.

He's helped me understand that what I provide, in terms of a service, has value to my customers.

I've just hired an employee. Steve helped me with that too. He helped in terms of how, because when I started my business, I thought I would work completely on my own. But it soon got the point where I was going to have to start looking outside, otherwise I would have to close the business because I couldn't do it all. So he helped me understand, well, if I was going to hire someone, whom did I need? You know, someone to clean the house, or a technical support person? Or should it be a salesperson? So he helped me identify the type of person I needed. He then gave me lots of advice on how to structure the employment contract so that it works for me as an employer. This was great because many employee's contracts, as you know, are very much in the employee's favour. He gave me a lot of hints and techniques in terms of how to structure the employment contract. And when I had my lawyer review the contract, he thought it was brilliant!

Before coaching started, I didn't even have a financial target. So once we got started, Steve talked to me about the four quadrants; about things that are urgent, things that are important, things that are not important, and things that are not urgent. And he had me spend a bit of time looking at how I was spending my time. Turns out I was doing many things that were not important, but urgent. And those things tended to be customer's demands. What I needed to do to make the business run better and more profitably was to reassess all this. So he's changed how I'm going to spend my day. I'm still not saying I'm doing it right, but right now I'm just trying to make it day-by-day, while all this other stuff's going on. But what I can see is the light at the end of the tunnel, whereas before I started coaching, I couldn't even see that.

Our plan tends to be a bit of a moving feast at present. One of the things I agreed to in our last session was that I would go back through my previous goal sheets (that I fill out prior to having a coaching session) to see if they're still valid. If I haven't achieved them, I'd decide if they're still important, and if so, I'd actually put a time on them.

Here's another thing Steve helped me with: I actually 'resigned' a customer! I sacked this customer I didn't want to work with any more. And it was so hard! Man. I thought, "I owe it to them" and he said, "But you don't deserve to be treated that way." And he actually let me get over that hurdle of, "My gosh, I can actually get rid of a client who doesn't respect me and who doesn't treat me well." In the end I'm so glad I did, because they got into all kinds of trouble and are now out of business. I'm so glad that I wasn't part of all that trouble they had after I resigned them. And I think that they were probably shocked receiving that letter from me; hearing that I didn't want to work with them any more.

Steve actually held my hand (not literally) through this whole process. I mean, I was shaking as I typed the letter, and shaking as I put it into the envelope, but you know, he just said, "You just have to do it. Do it." And I just closed my eyes and put blind faith in what he said. In the end it was very right to do it.

And now, I could do it again if I have to. He taught me that if you can do it once, you can do it again. He often says you get the customers you deserve. And that's one thing that I've found really valuable to keep in my mind. When I look back at the customers I have now, I just appreciate them all so much because I think I've started to attract, or draw, those people that I want to have as customers, instead of just having a customer for the sake of having one. So, by Steve saying, "You get the customers you deserve," it has become a self-fulfilling prophecy.

The Coach's Story

From the start, it was clear that Mary Sue had a strong belief in her service and product, and that she was knowledgeable and professional. And the business had great potential to grow, develop and meet her needs, personally and financially. So, why was it so difficult? When she came to me, everything was 'too hard' – clients were being difficult, not paying and not treating her with any respect - I mean they were being openly disrespectful to her.

From a coach's viewpoint, I recognised that to move beyond these issues we had to look inside, rather than focus on the results we were seeing outside. I realised that significant growth would come when she created a new and stronger identity that would support Mary Sue. When she had as much respect for herself as others did, then her business would grow and develop in the ways she was looking for.

We identified a number of areas to work in first, including:

- Creating a new identity.

- Sacking a client she no longer wanted to deal with.

- Changing her billing philosophy – and actually billing for work done.

- Increasing turnover and profits.

From the outset, Mary Sue listened, questioned, learned and did as she was told! As a client she's a pleasure to work with. When we began working on her identity I made a few suggestions, and helped determine the direction she could work on, and even suggested other people to talk to. She simply went off and did it. I think, because of the insights she received then, and because of how valuable it was for her, she was willing to trust me fairly quickly, so that when it became necessary to do some things that really frightened her, she just trusted me and went ahead and did them.

We started by realigning Mary Sue's belief in herself and correctly valuing her professional services. She learned that it was realistic and critical to charge a fair and profitable rate, and to charge it for all the work she does for a client. We put her rate up, and we ensured that all her work was charged. With that in place and turnover responding to the increased focus on sales, we decided to deal with a client who was causing her a great deal of concern. The client was (unfairly) blaming her for their situation, which also involved a third party, and rather than working towards a solution, the situation was heading for a breakdown. With my help, Mary Sue took leadership and facilitated an opportunity to resolve the issue, and once that was under way she advised the client that they were sacked – she did not wish to work with them any more. Although it was hard for her to do, she did what was required and as a result, professionally extracted herself from a difficult and potentially costly situation. And, she learned that she could choose her clients, as well as sack them if they were not willing to play nicely.

With the personal growth and the increasing performance of the business, we started looking at creating leverage for her, so she could do more without having to work longer or harder. Soon after she identified the characteristics of the person she wanted to work with, an excellent candidate turned up. He had years of ACT! experience, and was personable, presentable and professional. Although he was living in the US, he wanted to come to New Zealand to live, so it seemed too good to be true. Mary Sue made a decision to trust her instincts, and I coached her in developing an offer, a contract, and securing the new team member's services. Over the past month, since he has been on board, every week has been a record of increasing sales. And, he has also earned great feedback from clients, so Achieve! is now being seen as the supplier of choice, with technical support and service being the best available locally.

Although we've surpassed all of the original goals, Mary Sue continues to work with me. Our coaching goals have changed and now we are looking at how to create an asset from the business. And, how we can further leverage the business so that she can focus on doing just the things she wants to do and do them well. She now has vision and clarity around where she is going, along with the knowledge that she is already getting there. That's one of those things that have made it such a great experience for me working with Mary Sue. Being part of the growth and development of the business and also personally, and now taking all that to a new level. The next year will be even more exciting than this year, and I know that Achieve! will become more and more the business Mary Sue wants.

The Outcome

Mary Sue has achieved so much in the short time she has received coaching. Much of this has been in the non-tangible aspects of business – things that are so important to very small business operations. But let her explain:

"I don't feel isolated and alone any more. I'm married to a guy with a PhD, he's very smart, he's a scientist, he's a carbohydrate chemist, but to try and talk to him about business issues like this, he can't really relate to it. I don't have colleagues around me that I can sit down with to complain about the boss. I'm completely on my own, and my German Shepherd, she just doesn't understand when I complain! So suddenly I just don't feel alone anymore. I've got a shoulder to cry on, or someone I can ring up and say, you know, "I don't know what I'm doing!" He'll always take a few minutes to talk to me."

Yes, Business Coaches provide support in a wide range of areas, all of which are vital to today's business owners. And it's important to realise that every case is different. Every Coach has a unique set of strengths and challenges. They also have a wide ranging knowledge base from which to draw, so they can, for instance, match a solution that worked in a particular business to a challenge faced by another business in a different industry. But they're not just sales experts or management gurus. They can become a human resources manager or distribution specialist to a small business. But let's not interrupt Mary Sue.

"I now understand my worth – and my business' worth. I've just doubled my human resources. I now bill, and bill a good amount, for the work I do. My new employee is absolutely brilliant, in terms of what he's done in a week and a half and the revenue that he's generating. My Coach has helped me through these things. And just to reiterate, he's helped me to identify the kind of customers that I want to have; the kind of people I want to have in my life."

The Business Coach also provides focus to the business owner. This is an area that Mary Sue has benefited greatly. So what is she working on at the moment?

"This urgent vs. important issue. Taking the time to be able to build the business as opposed to just chasing after customers needs all the time. I now have a vision for what I want the business to be and for so many months I just forgot about that vision and thought, 'OK, I'll just try and get through the next few days.' I can picture what I want the company to be. I can see it out there."

So, what vision does she now have for the future?

"I don't imagine I'll ever part company with Steve, my Business Coach. I think there's always going to be a need for somebody like him, especially when you're the boss, you know, where else do you go? I want to run a successful business with about 3 or 4, maybe 5, team members located in downtown Wellington, providing national service to customers in not only Act!, but other software programmes as well. You know, not focusing on how you move your mouse from here to here to get this kind of end result, but why do you do it. And that could be how to improve internal communications, improve sales, reduce stress and workload, or how to make the business more effective.

"I'd like to be in a position where I could actually sell the business and have that freedom, because right now ... A while ago, I asked, "I wonder what my business is worth?" Steve said, "Well find out." And so I did some investigation and I found that it was worth very little. If I were to sell it, it would be worth nothing because I am it. Going through that little exercise really made me change my thinking. I think I was trying to take credit for what I did, but now I just change my wording and Achieve! takes credit for what is done. You know, there's a real difference there. And Steve helped me identify that. I couldn't say, 'Mary Sue achieved this,' it has to be, 'Achieve! achieved that goal for this customer.' I think I was probably doing that for egotistical reasons, but I've changed that because one day I do want to be able to sell the business; you know I do want to be able to play tennis during the day or whatever it is I want to do!

"I think that whenever anyone starts a new business, they get their lawyer and an accountant, but they should also get a Business Coach. I think that if you consider the high attrition rate of new businesses – how many go under in the first 2 or 3 years – I probably would also have gone under if I didn't have Steve here to help me through. I would have said, 'Oh, it's too much! I think I'd rather be an employee!' He's actually been the one to help me stay in business and actually grow it, instead of giving up on it. I think the world of him!"

▌ Landmark Restaurant Uncovers New Potential

Markets change, tastes change, so the companies and the individuals who choose to compete in those markets must change.

~ An Wang ~

The Business

Name: Rendezvous Hock Lock Kee Restaurant

Address: #02-02/03 Hotel Rendezvous, Gourmet Gallery, 9 Bras Basah Road, Singapore, 189559

Owner: Seah King Ming

Type Of Business: Restaurant

Business Sector: Food & Beverage/Service

Established: 1950

Coach: Theodore Chuang

The Challenge

Usually it's only small, struggling businesses that most people imagine would have need of a Business Coach. After all, aren't they the ones that have little expertise or business acumen? Aren't they the ones that think they know it all, and then find out that they actually don't?

Whilst it's probably true that many business people who engage a Business Coach do so precisely because they've come to realise that their lack of training or knowledge in running a business is costing them dearly. Having survived, and prospered, for many years doesn't necessarily mean a business is immune to failure. Having survived those first few critical years doesn't guarantee success at all. And it certainly doesn't mean there's nothing more to be learned.

Landmark Restaurant Uncovers New Potential

Take Rendezvous Hock Lock Kee Restaurant in Singapore, for instance. Here's a well-established business that is celebrating its 52nd anniversary this year. Well, the business has actually been around a lot longer than that. You see, some 70 years ago, the present owner's father, Mr Seah Soo Khoon opened a coffee shop called Hock Lock Kee on the corner of Princep Street and Bras Basah Road and it was there that British troops stationed in Singapore began to hang out. It soon became known as the Rendezvous Restaurant. Then, some 10 years ago Mr Seah King Ming took over the family business from his father. These days the restaurant is located within an upper class hotel (Hotel Rendezvous) that was actually named after the restaurant! The restaurant is decorated with old photographs so customers are taken on a trip down memory lane every time they visit. The ambiance is one of nostalgia; customers can step back in time as they enjoy one of the most tempting arrays of gastronomic Western Sumatran cuisine in all of Singapore.

Tourists and business travellers stay in the hotel, and there are some high-class private residences within a 500m radius of the restaurant, with offices and shops making up the remainder of the immediate area. As a result, the restaurant caters mainly to middle class (and above) income earners. These are mostly families, businessmen and white-collar workers, but a small percentage of customers are, of course, tourists. The restaurant is famous for its good customer service, personal touches and the superb quality of their authentic dishes. The restaurant is well-known within the local community, especially among older folk who are convinced that if the restaurant has remained in business this long, it must be authentic and credible.

I think you get the picture. This is not your average eat-it-and-beat-it joint.

So how were they doing, financially? They were coping very well. In fact, they had been able to consistently meet all their targets. If that were so, what could a Business Coach do for them, then? A whole lot, as you're about to discover.

The Moment Of Truth

The old saying that you're never too old to learn is very true. And I guess in this case it could be broadened to mean you're never too experienced to stop learning. What prompted Mr Seah King Ming to seek professional help was his strong desire to acquire sales and marketing knowledge. You see, his business goals at the time were simply to improve the business' performance.

He had determined that the business could do more marketing to generate leads, and as a result he needed more marketing knowledge. He was having difficulties creating and implementing new marketing strategies for the business, and he also faced some challenges getting his team to constantly follow serving routines. Some team members, being less educated, couldn't communicate well with English-speaking customers, and were therefore, having difficulty building rapport with them. However, he treasures the loyalty of these long-serving team members as much as they treasure him.

He came into contact with coach Theodore Chuang through a telemarketer.

The Coach's Story

Walking into the restaurant on the day I was to carry out a diagnosis of the business gave me an unusual feeling. Just by the look of the restaurant itself, I could see that it was indeed very different from other restaurants. It was spick and span and the staff greeted me with a warm smile. I thoroughly enjoyed looking at the photos of old Singapore that adorn the walls. I felt like I was taken back in time. It reminded me of my grandfather's coffee shop where I spent a fair bit of my childhood years. The only difference was that this place was really clean and cosy.

The owner came out and greeted me warmly. Quickly, he offered me a drink. My first impression of him was of a mild-mannered and cultured businessman who conducts business fairly. And I got to find out more about this during the program. He treasures his staff and doesn't favour retrenchment. During the business diagnostic, he appeared to be quite comfortable with the way his business was going. It was soon revealed that he had met all his goals since the day he took charge of the business. And that was some 10 years ago! Probing further, I got to realise that he wanted to improve the business and was willing to learn. Of course, the *ACTION* coaching programme is all about learning and gaining knowledge, and this I stressed to him. He requested time to consider and to go through the different program details that I left him.

Our new business relationship commenced one week later.

The Alignment Report got him to revisit his personal and business goals. It also made him aware of the business challenges that confronted him and highlighted a number of ways to overcome them. The process got him to analyse his target market and think about his market awareness. The first decision taken was to put new sales and marketing strategies in place. This was because the restaurant was not doing much in the way of sales and marketing activities at that point, and the owner realised he had to get some outside help if he wanted to commence moving down this path. Fortunately, he didn't find this traumatic, as he had already decided he wanted to progress and improve.

At the beginning of coaching, the goal was to improve revenue by 10% by the end of the program.

I then devised a recommended Plan of *ACTION* – which consisted manly of sales and marketing strategies within the five areas of leverage (leads, conversion rate, number of transaction, average dollar sale and margins).

Landmark Restaurant Uncovers New Potential

We certainly faced some challenges along the way. These included time and capability constraints faced by the owner, when it came to copywriting and implementation, as he didn't have anyone to help him. And he didn't plan to have anyone doing that full-time for him, either.

How were they overcome? I helped him with the first copy and the rest were outsourced. We also worked on Host Beneficiary and Strategic Alliance strategies to increase the restaurant's leverage, as this was more cost effective than hiring a dedicated marketing person.

Of the novel solutions we introduced, the most successful was the Food Of The Month Promotion. The offer was to give a FREE desert for a dish that takes at least two people to consume. So sales of desert also increased for that month, and all for the cost of one promotion and a once-off printing cost for the posters!

The Outcome

The restaurant has achieved fantastic results due to the efforts of Theodore Chuang. As an example, during the restaurant's Food Of The Month Promotion in September 2002, (a delicious curry fishhead dish), sales improved by 100%. After the promotion had ended, sales were up on previous months by 75%. It looks like the product has found a new benchmark for average sales.

The test of the pudding is in the eating, as the old saying goes. So what results were achieved the next time the promotion was run? In October, the Food Of The Month was chicken korma, and sales were again up by 75%. The owner was impressed, as normally customers would choose chicken rendang instead of a chicken meat dish.

Mr Seah King Ming has discovered his hidden talents in sales and marketing through Business Coaching. He says, " The program helps to widen your mind on the many sides of sales and marketing. It provides a better analysis of your business strategies and brings out your hidden capabilities. The *ACTION* program has opened up many interesting aspects of sales and marketing strategies, most of which I now find relatively easy to implement. Without the programme I would have thought the strategies difficult and time consuming. Despite my apprehension at the beginning, we have achieved what we set out to achieve and I am very pleased with the sales results."

▌ Pest Control Company's Success Sends Shock Waves Through Industry

---

I am the world's worst salesman, therefore,
I must make it easy for people to buy.

~ F. W. Woolworth ~

The Business

Name: Ridpest Sdn Bhd

Address: No. 7 Jalan Wangsa Setia 1, Wangsa Melawati, 53300 Kuala Lumpur, Wilayah Persekutuan, Malaysia

Owner: Stephen Liu

Type Of Business: Pest Control Management Services

Business Sector: Service

Established: 1985

Coach: Yow Feng Hing

The Challenge

Many business owners choose business coaching as a strategy to achieve various desired outcomes. But sometimes achieving these outcomes can have unforseen consequences. This is exactly what happened to this Malaysian pest control company.

Even though the business was well established, and well regarded in the market, the time came when its owner realised his business knowledge needed updating. He was concerned that, even though his business was doing OK, he was having less and less time for himself as the months went by.

He wanted practical information, not loads of theory. But let him tell his story.

Stephen's Story

I had been working in the pest control industry for many years. Technically speaking, I was very competent. Nevertheless, I knew that, however, good I was, there was a limit to what I could achieve in terms of remuneration. This prompted me to venture out on my own, so I started a pest control business in 1985. I thought and believed that through business, I could have more money, more freedom and a higher standard of living.

My business had been enjoying a steady and gradual growth since its inception. Nothing spectacular. I had always faced the challenges of improving my sales and profits. But as my business continued to expand, I encountered even more challenges, particularly in leading and motivating my team to perform at consistently higher levels of service. Plus, I was getting busier by the day. Instead of having more personal time, I had to spend even more time in my business.

I soon realized that my knowledge base was not sufficient to cope with the ever-increasing demands posed by my business. I then decided to complete a diploma course in management and update my knowledge regarding the latest technological trends and new developments in the pest management field through reading industry magazines. However, there was not much I could tap into as far as practical sales and marketing information was concerned.

The Moment Of Truth

All that changed when I received a call from Mr Yow Feng Hing, a Business Coach from *ACTION International*. Usually, I would not speak to any salesperson that cold-called me. However, his approach impressed me greatly.

He happened to visit a trade show that my business was participating in. Upon receiving a thank you letter from me, he called to express his appreciation. At the same time he disclosed his identity and said he could offer me some tips on improving my marketing efforts further. I was intrigued and decided to grant him an appointment. In hindsight, this appointment marked the beginning of a new milestone for my business.

During the one-hour Diagnostic Consultation, I discovered so many things that I didn't know. I then realized that although I may be a competent technician, I was certainly not a good marketer.

I remember vividly one question he asked me. "Could you utter in one short paragraph why people should do business with you?" I was dumbfounded. I had no answer to that.

I was further astounded when he shared with me the true definition of a business. It is a commercial, profitable enterprise that works without me.

Pest Control Company's Success Sends Shock Waves Through Industry

It had never occurred to me that a true business has to be one that runs without my presence. It really blew my mind.

I then decided to engage him as my personal Business Coach, though with some reservations. My business partner (also my wife) was even more concerned. However, her impression changed drastically after joining in a few coaching sessions. She got so excited after the business experienced some tangible results that she described Yow as being 'God-sent' to help us in our business.

In the past, I used to generate business from the Yellow Pages, leaflets, referrals from clients, staff and friends and, occasionally, press ads. Nothing different from what my competitors did. However, I couldn't pinpoint systematically the amount of business contributed by each source but I thought the Yellow Pages would be the greatest contributor.

However, with **ACTION International's** help, I started to test and measure the various sources that were producing leads in a very systematic and scientific way. To my surprise, a very negligible number actually came from the Yellow Pages. I decided to discontinue the Yellow Pages ad, which was in actual fact an expense to me, thanks to the testing and measuring system that my **ACTION** Business Coach taught me.

At the same time, I could also measure the conversion rates being achieved by my salespeople. Extra training was provided to beef up their performances – and I could see improvement.

Amongst the many things that my Business Coach recommended and taught me, the most phenomenal was helping me to coin a very powerful Unique Selling Preposition (USP) for my business – "Guaranteed to eliminate termites, or your money back." This really put us head and shoulders above our competitors.

Never did I imagine it would be so powerful that it would actually send shock waves through the whole industry. Some of the industry players were so rattled that they didn't know what to do. They couldn't come up with any responsive strategy to counter our new marketing campaign.

But that wasn't the only powerful and remarkable thing my business experienced – there were two more, and I was astounded by the spectacular results they achieved. Firstly, Yow taught me how to set up a 'host-beneficiary' with a club. I invested RM4,075 in total and at last count, the extra sales I generated was RM27,250 – an amazing 668.7% return. Secondly, he went one step further by helping me to rewrite my advertisement. I used to regularly receive 10 to 15 calls from it, but with the new ad, I generated 131 enquiries that contributed an extra RM80,220 to my business. And as my investment was only RM2,494, that's a whopping 3,216% return. More sensational results are on the way …

The Coach's Story

During the Diagnostic and Alignment Consultations, I came to realize that Stephen did not know the points of difference that his business stood for. I then taught him how to come up with a powerful USP, and as there was no pest control company in the country that had ever offered their customers a 100% money back refund, this seemed like the ideal point of difference. Just by having this strategy in place, their salespeople found it easier to convert prospects, even though their prices were not the lowest inthe market.

From their latest financial figures, their annual turnover has jumped by an impressive 60%. I believe a great part of this can be attributed to their new USP.

The other area that I helped Stephen to work on was his advertisement. As usual, the ad was a typical 'tombstone' ad. I taught him how to increase its response rate just by changing it into a 'direct response' type ad. Just that simple twist helped pull in 131 responses, contributing an extra RM80,220 to their business. The normal response rate was between 10 and 15 calls.

Above all, I believe a great part of Stephen's resounding success is due to his open-mind and willingness to test and measure any idea and strategy introduced to him. In fact, mind set was the very first thing I did with him - right at the beginning of the coaching session. No amount of business development could come about without any positive mental development.

The other positive thing that Stephen did was that he read any book that I recommended. That definitely helped accelerate his learning.

The Outcome

I'm sure you'll agree, this is a spectacular result. Aren't those figures sensational? But for the wrap-up, let's go back to Stephen Liu.

"I believed Yow, my **ACTION** Business Coach, could help me to explore and unearth even more goldmines in my business in the days to come. The ideas that he taught me were basically common sense; there was no rocket science. One idea actually germinated another. The books that he recommended further accelerated the learning process.

"What is most important was that he inculcated in me the right mindset with which to look at business. This really helped a lot.

"Besides, as a coach, he could actually see some of the flaws inherent in my business. He provided another pair of eyes with which I could objectively view my business.

Pest Control Company's Success Sends Shock Waves Through Industry

"I have benefited so much from the coaching service that without any hesitationI would recommend it to any business owners who have a strong desire to grow their businesses.

"Yes, the fees may be high, but it is relatively cheap compared to the returns you'll get …

"I've no regrets whatsoever in engaging Yow as my Business Coach. In fact, I wish he had come along earlier."

▌ Even Coaches Need Coaching ... Here's One That Loves To Be Coached

---

A business that makes nothing but money is a poor kind of business.

- Henry Ford -

The Business

Name: FarSight Ltd

Address: 22-410 The Esplanade, Island Bay, Wellington, New Zealand

Owner: Jonathan Black

Type Of Business: Organisational Psychologist

Business Sector: Service

Established: Originally started in 1996, re-branded and incorporated in 2002

Coach: Steve McDonald

The Challenge

Ever thought about who a hairdresser goes to to have her hair cut? Or where a mechanic has his car serviced? But what about someone who coaches business people? Good question, huh?

Yet when you think about it, they're no different to any other type of business. They also have needs and requirements, just like any other. And they usually can benefit from having an outside, non-partial and totally objective perspective on where they're heading as a business, what they could be doing better and how they can go about improving their performance.

The example I'm now going to tell you about now concerns just such a business. And it's an interesting one, because it was built around a particular philosophy or outlook on life that is fundamental to its very existence. It involves ethics, passion and lifestyle, as much as it does good old-fashioned business. And it challenges accepted views of the business world by its industry. It's a great story – I love it and hope you do too ...

This business is an organisational psychology practice called Farsight. Farsight is based in Wellington, and delivers a variety of services to the corporate sector, individuals, teams and large businesses, particularly in the area of personnel selection.

They give a lot of occupational health advice, personal coaching, and some counselling, and deliver specialist training on stress, trauma, team building, managing dangerous clients, and critical incident management.

It's a home business basically for lifestyle reasons, which means that their overheads are low and they don't need to pass those costs on to their clients. While many clients like to come to their premises, others are quite happy to be visited at their workplace.

FarSight prefers to steer clear of the conventional office, preferring to base themselves in a converted suburban home. The stainless steel, glass frontage look, with a receptionist at the front, isn't for them. Their philosophy is that the workplace must be a fun and healthy place.

Do they have an average client? Yes, they do. Their average client is, generally speaking, the manager of a medium or large-sized organisation who would be looking at delivering some kind of service. They'd be interested in a training package or a selection of services and, typically, this would be in reaction to something that had gone wrong. You know, like having to replace a team member or facing a crisis in staff performance or health.

The size of the organisations they deal with is usually somewhere around the 200+ mark, although they do prefer working with smaller teams than that because then they can work with the whole organisation and really make powerful changes.

OK, you've got the picture. Let's hear what the owner has to say.

Jonathan's Story

The company was incorporated in March this year but to borrow the term from Charles Handy, it's really the second growth curve. It was really a company change and re-branding of the original company that I established in 1996 as a part-time exercise. So Farsight was incorporated in March 2002 to become a full-time and professional structure with which we can service our client needs and, at the same time, expand throughout Australasia.

For background to the business problem, I think I can look at it in two ways. If I'm looking at what growth is like now compared to what it was before coaching started, it has increased, I would say, 2 or 3-fold. This was primarily through some very subtle marketing and personal contacts – getting the name out there, meeting people, getting the brand out there, and things like that.

In terms of the bigger picture, we're still very small and that reflects a number of things – only now are we starting to get into marketing ... but I'm also determined to focus on the brand and the knowledge of that brand. I don't want something that immediately rolls of people's lips (without a knowledge of what it means) but something that roll of the lips of people who are our target market.

The target audience will be professionals in the same community, because word of mouth is the most powerful from of marketing. I have a very, very firm philosophy about working as part of a team. There's plenty of work out there, but the market needs to be educated. I like to be very, very good to other people and to help them in business.

The main challenges I faced before meeting Steve McDonald were 2-fold: one was the lack of structure – the lack of a plan, and the second was a lack of inertia.

I think why I went along with Steve was an acknowledgement that from a business perspective, that was what I needed to kick Farsight off the ground and get things up and running with a level of steam of its own. That was one of the reasons why I went to Steve.

I needed a catalyst to do that and I recognised it. My professional training is in psychology; I understand the benefit of coaching quite well, so I had no doubt. It was really a catalyst for putting a plan in place, and by acting on that plan, to create a level of inertia. Priorities were made, goals were achieved, things were measured and progress was made. When I look back, there's actually no question whatsoever that, whilst I might have been able to slave away to get to this position from where I was 12 months ago, it's highly, highly unlikely that I would have done so.

I'm on my own. I do intend to build-up without any doubt, but it's the usual story that every business starts out small and you can't afford to bring people on board straight away. People usually want to be part of a concern that's got a decent client base to give them some security of income, before they come on board, and I can quite understand that.

We all spend an awful lot of time, when we start up a business, chasing our tails and with a good business system in place, you can reduce a lot of the stress and significantly reduce some of the time you spend growing the business. That doesn't mean you're going to be working a 40-hour week; you're not. You're going to be working a lot more than that, but there's a difference between a 60 and an 80-hour week. You know, I don't want to be re-inventing the wheel every time it comes to paying GST (Goods and Services Tax) and I'm scrambling around trying to find my receipts. Basically with financial systems, contact plans, and the like in place, you can rather invest your time in growing the business and building relationships or in making products or whatever your strength happens to be.

So it's an awful lot of time, certainly, and it affects your work-life balance without any doubt whatsoever. And that's an area I'm very passionate about. But it doesn't have to be that way. To a degree, I think in a lot of start-up businesses it occurs, because people are unwilling to recognise the benefit of learning easier and more effective ways of doing things.

Steve has had a positive effect on the work-life balance I have. That has been primarily through setting up systems and getting things in place, setting goals and measuring progress. I often think that as a small businessperson, you try to do everything and then you get to a point where you wonder, 'How am I going? What am I doing?' You become very reactive and need to be able to sit down and think, 'Hold on, what is the health of my business? What needs to be in place?'

Before I met Steve, the business definitely wasn't meeting the financial targets I was hoping for. I'm now forecasting a 300% increase in revenue compared to the last financial year.

Now partly that's due to Steve's efforts and partly due to other factors as well. But Steve certainly helped tremendously by putting those systems in place and he has certainly had a key role in making that easier than it would have otherwise been.

The Moment of Truth

I wouldn't say there was a particular event that caused me to take on a Business Coach; it was rather a series of circumstances that occurred over a couple of years. But I also think recognition of my limitations, particularly as I'm a professional trainer in a helping profession, not being traditionally trained in business skills and having a middle-class background, as well as an altruistic streak helped steer me that way.

The reality is when you are building a business, you need to sell. You need to be able to do marketing; you need to be able to get out there and sell your service, product or whatever. Yet, I come from a profession that fundamentally thinks money's the dark side of the force and I'm quite serious about that. I keep 'rarking' up my colleagues and they think I'm Darth Vader sometimes (I think), but it's true. There's nothing wrong with selling and making a profit and even a psychologist sometimes needs help working through that. There's nothing wrong with marketing.

I had a personal realisation about my value system. I always knew it was there. But I was also thinking, 'Who can help me through this?'

I tried to work through it myself, but there's only so much self-therapy you can do in front of the mirror every morning before you realise, 'Well, this isn't working.' And you can do a lot of stuff yourself through reading, through talking with friends, and basically through being open-minded, but unfortunately there's not actually that many people who are that open-minded! And Steve was very beneficial.

Even Coaches Need Coaching ... Here's One That Loves To Be Coached

I think one of the most valuable lessons he taught me was how to change my view of a salesperson. Often in our society we are raised to think of a car salesperson when we think of a salesperson. The concept of selling is like going door-to-door or cold selling; you know, the hard selling of the car salesperson, and that's not what it is at all.

And the way he helped me through that was to say that what I'm doing is helping people make a professional decision to choose, and that's exactly it. And you're right, that is a value system. How do you work through that? Often, I think, many small business owners totally underestimate their values in terms of the importance they have. Small businesses, and here I'm talking about 1 or 2 people or a married couple, don't realise that while they may have great technical skills and ideas, they just don't have great business skills.

It was important to me to meet someone who could work with me to create a vision for myself of how I could sell ethically.

Steve and I are members of Business Network International, Harbour City Chapter, here in Wellington and that's how I met him. He's very vibrant, very positive, and very passionate about what he does, and passion is a key word for me. I've got a lot of respect for his business skills and knowledge.

Yeah, there are some challenges. I think the biggest challenge is to keep going. You know, getting to the point where you think, 'God, I want a day off.' That is the challenge; that's the biggest challenge in that work-life balance. The other biggest challenge is keeping the faith ... to keep the faith in what your passion and your vision is, and to keep going, because you get tired; you get fatigued. I think that another big challenge for me is to keep maintaining the self-discipline to keep setting goals and to keep the measuring going. And sometimes I'm a bit slack on that, but I always get it done.

The method I use to overcome these challenges is to turn to people to discuss business. I inspire them and that's when I turn around and say, 'Well maybe I just need to do a bit better.'

That's really the way I've been dealing with it. And from time-to-time, yes, I will turn to Steve for help. For example, I'm purchasing some specialist advice from him at the moment; a business plan, and that's incredibly valuable, but on a day-to-day, week-to-week basis, generally speaking it would be others that I approach – friends, colleagues and other business owners. I generally find that I will talk to others, and in talking to them, I will inspire myself. But basically, if you set the standard and tell people you're going to do it, basically you've made a commitment and if you don't, you're going to be terribly embarrassed. I use that as motivation.

The Coach's Story

When I began working with Jonathan, his business concept was starting to take shape, and he needed guidance as to how to clarify his vision and purpose. He also needed assistance with motivation and direction to get the business moving forward. He had a sound concept and good technical skills, and that needed to be coupled with momentum, advice and accountability.

Jonathan attended a networking function at which I spoke about the purpose and value of having a Business Coach.

Once I started working with him, I suggested we focus on his purpose, and developing sales and business management skills. I also suggested we establish a business plan, including a marketing plan and business development guidelines.

My plan of action was to work initially through group coaching sessions that would be followed-up with consulting services to focus on specific things such as marketing, client communication strategies and a business development plan.

All client communications, both written and personal, as well as product packaging and presentation, were tested and measured.

Changes made to the business or the owner's routine included setting aside allocated time to plan and develop the business, writing a business plan, devising a timeline for engaging investor and technical partners, and creating an investment business plan.

The Outcome

Jonathan is now far more directed, confident and motivated. He has a clearer view of where he and the business are at now, where they are going, how they will get there and when that is likely to be.

He has achieved much in a short space of time.

"I think I've achieved direction," Jonathan said. "I've achieved a sense of purpose. I've achieved a timeline. I've got some strategic goals regarding where I want the company to go and the size I want to grow it to. And I've got greater clarification of the services I want the company to deliver."

Notice how all his achievements are in the strategic area rather than in the financial area of facts and figures.

"And what's just as important to me, I've got greater clarification about what the company needs. It's not about me; it's about the company. At the end of the day, in 5 years time, I might be interested in selling it, and that's fine, but I don't want the value of the company to be affected by whether or not I'm there or whether or not

Even Coaches Need Coaching ... Here's One That Loves To Be Coached

I'm standing in the room training; it's the company with the perceived value, not my name, and I can recommend that."

Coaching doesn't always have to be about only improving the bottom line, although every result will indirectly have an affect on the profitability of the business. In this case, the primary focus was on all the 'intangible' things that so often confuse and mystify business owners. Clarifying the very reason a business exists can often be something the owner has never even thought about. Sure, to make a living, but then one would be better off getting a job. Motivation, accountability, focus and an impartial point-of-view are often just as important as developing new lead generation strategies or ways to increase the average number of transactions each customer makes.

"So a lot of the value that I received from coaching has been to do with those fundamental concepts. At the moment I'm setting it up for the future. Revenue streams and business tools ... but basically, I'm keeping the commitment with Steve because I actually enjoy it."

Get that? He actually enjoys the coaching experience. Business is supposed to be fun. And why shouldn't it be? You spend enough time at it, so enjoy it. Ever noticed that I call business a game? Well I do, and for good reason. But let's get back to Jonathan. Let's hear more about what, in his view, the results of his coaching program were.

"I will never finish working with Steve, mainly because even when I'm successful, I would like him to come back in and celebrate that success ... I think that's very important. It's a personal philosophy, and part of the reason I set up in business is personal philosophy. You know, at the end of the day, I want to write some books. I hear this all the time: 'There's nothing out there for us; everything's got a European and American flavour.' There's nothing wrong with that, but there's no New Zealand or Australian analogy for business, and it would be great to expose and celebrate that.

"What would it look like if I were successful? I would have a passive income of $50,000 per year; I would be contributing to the employment of other people; and I would have a good business and client base in both New Zealand and Australia. We have a commitment in our company to be giving back 5% a year to the community. Now I know that's not free, of course – we get a marketing value from it, but it's still nice.

"What I have is a vision of sustainable equity, where I don't have to work but I choose to. I want to continue to contribute, not just to the financial health of the organisation, but also to the emotional health of the employees and the people associated with the company.

"I want people to be associated with Farsight and to enjoy being associated with it. I want people who work for us to enjoy that. I want the employees to enjoy coming to work every day. And that may sound like a hard ask, but it's an attitudinal thing.

We're talking about occupational health, we're not talking about money – we're talking about attitude, style, demeanour and the way that we work.

"I want people to be able to feel that they can chill out if they come up and say, "Today I just want to chill; I want to chill out."

"I want to be in a position, for example, where I can reward staff by saying I don't want people to work 5-day weeks. I think it's inherently unhealthy! I really do. I think there are other things to do in life. And I realise more and more, too, from my personal experience and professional practice, that many people would love to work 4 days a week, as long as they felt secure – as long as it would give them a reasonable income so they could meet their needs and obligations. Well, why not? I'd love to be able to pay someone to go to the gym twice a week. Take care of yourself; take care of your body! You know, I guess it would be a different way of working; a different way of doing things.

"So I have some very, very big ambitions and I'm very, very keen if the opportunity arises to have others share in that particular celebration. I will always be turning to Steve from time-to-time, no doubt about it.

"You've got to have passion. And now I've got to find some way of putting that vision into practice. Well, I can put it into practice myself, but it's about bringing other people along with me, and I've got some ideas about doing that and I love it! We take life far too seriously – we really, really do. We have so much fear and it's totally unnecessary."

▌ Beauty Therapist Survives Staff Walkout And Prospers

The employer generally gets the employees he deserves.

~ Walter Gilbey

The Business

Name: Indulge Beauty Therapy Ltd

Address: Level 1, Kirkcaldie & Stains, Lambton Quay, Wellington, New Zealand

Owner: Angeline Knapp

Type Of Business: Beauty Therapy

Business Sector: Service

Purchased: 2000

Coach: Steve McDonald

The Challenge

Having the wrong people on your team is one thing, but managing to survive when they all leave can be quite another. This is what happened to Angeline Knapp, who runs a beauty therapy business in Wellington, New Zealand.

Her business survived. Why? Because she had a business coach to help her weather the storm.

You see, one of the most delicate competencies required by any small business owner is that of handling people. This should not be surprising, as there has been much made over the years about how customers should be treated. Remember the saying, "The Customer Is Always Right?" Here we're talking about your external stakeholders, but what about your internal stakeholders – the members of your team?

Beauty Therapist Survives Staff Walkout And Prospers

Being able to effectively interact with your own team has got to be one of the most over-looked aspects of business today. You see, most business owners are so focused on what's going on outside their businesses – in their markets – that they simply forget what's happening inside them.

Small businesses that have the luxury of having more than just the owner working in it, find that each team member begins to play a vital role in the operations of that business. They become key players. And the business typically doesn't have the leeway necessary to soak-up unplanned fluctuations that happen from time-to-time such as, for example, when someone is off sick or on leave. Unless there are systems in place to cater for that, that is.

So let's have a closer look at what happened at Indulge Beauty Therapy. To begin with, they were a barely viable business. They were holding their own, but not really growing. The owner's beliefs and lack of business experience was holding the business back from being able to develop further. Financially the business was in the balance – some months were good and some were poor. This is a very typical small business scenario, I'm afraid.

Angeline's Story

Our business is Indulge Beauty Therapy and we're located on the first floor of Kirkcaldie and Stains in central Wellington. We provide a large range of beauty therapy treatments.

Our average client is 40 years old and over. Many of them are businesswomen while others don't work. They're mainly Kirkcaldie and Stains customers.

Since having Steve as our Business Coach, we're looking at slightly different customers now, and we don't target just anybody - we're being a bit more selective about who it is that we're after.

We've been in business for 4 years – we just celebrated our fourth birthday, in fact. There are two of us at the moment, both full-time, but I am looking for a third.

Our profile is growing. For quite a time we were situated behind a hair salon and only had one room, so we were very busy and couldn't really get any busier. So, I think people are a little bit more aware of us now because the hair salon's gone and we're a bit more visual, though not hugely so, and I think that word of mouth is definitely increasing.

We've put in another treatment room as well as a manicure room. We stock the 'Jessica' range of hand and feet products and are the only stockists in Wellington – it's from the United States and it's pretty well-known by anyone that's been to the UK, as well as being pretty big over in the United States. We've even had write-ups in the paper.

Anyway, I was working a lot and getting nowhere really. I had previously met another **ACTION International** business coach when I first started out in business, so I was aware of what **ACTION International** did and what we could achieve through working with them.

When I first started in business I was working 7 days a week, so that pretty much eliminated any time I had for myself. I did that for about 12 months. Financially, it was a bit of a struggle.

The Moment of Truth

I think it was when I had a break. I went to Australia for 9 days and thought I just had to make a go of it. I was getting pretty tired of doing what I'd been doing for 3 years.

Initially I tried to make a start with coaching but that sort of fell through. Later, I attended a Leverage Board Game evening and met quite a few different coaches and yeah, I quite liked Steve …

When he came to compile an Alignment Report, we talked about what it was that I wanted out of business and out of life, and what I was going to do in the areas that I thought needed improvement. He then went away and put the Alignment Report together. It took about 2 weeks to work out the different strategies that we could use as a basis to start off with.

At the time, I had two team members and they decided to leave within 6 weeks of each other. Yes, that was certainly a challenge, but you know, you work through it. Steve was very helpful. He kept my feet firmly on the ground. He made me look at it from a business point-of-view. And I'm really happy with the team I've got now. So it's actually worked out really well.

There's been a huge amount of stuff that we've implemented and put in place because of what happened (my people leaving); that has changed the way I look at things. A process – now there's a way that we do things as opposed to how we used to; you know; right, let's just do this now, and then that …

Well, normally when you first start working with a business coach, you don't initially start by looking at your team. We started with the team. You'd normally be looking at implementing a couple of bits and pieces and seeing how they go, but we needed to rebuild what it was that we had anyway. This actually turned out to be quite good.

I certainly do see that it's all coming together … we've got a plan and it's really good. You don't feel that you're just working and working and working.

The Coach's Story

Angeline had attended several *ACTION* events over the course of a year, and in fact had looked at coaching before, but had not been able to make the required commitment. She attended a Leverage Board Game evening I hosted and we made contact again after that, when she indicated that the time was right to make the commitment to a coaching program with me.

We initially needed to capitalise on the mindset of the owner to really get the business flying. Within a month of starting coaching, the 2 therapist employees resigned for various reasons, and we needed to put a new therapist on board. By using *ACTION'S* Team Recruitment process, we were able to focus on getting the right person first, then training them to acquire the required skills later. This resulted in having a much more suitable team member. Now we are building on this to set up a complete team of the right people.

In addition, the owner needed to develop better business knowledge so she could track the business' financials and profitability. By teaching her how to measure the business, the Key Performance Indicators and the critical numbers, she is now able to rapidly assess how she is going on a month-by-month basis. We are also working on installing Critical Non-Essentials, to help with the retention of customers by developing loyal customers, enhancing repeat business and generating referral business.

My plan of action was to first recruit the best people, then to systemise the operational tasks within the business. Everything was to be tested and measured. We would use regular customer communications, follow-up treatments, and initiate a new customer welcome package and newsletter. The plan also included the introduction and marketing of new product lines and specialised treatments, as well as to develop a customer database for special occasions and offers.

Changes were made to the business owner's routine. Business development time was allocated and blocked out – this was time to work on the business. She also now had to work to a plan for the development of the business. User systems were introduced to train, measure and manage the team's day-to-day activities. Systems for booking and for customer communications were also developed and implemented.

The Outcome

Notice how the implementation and use of systems have made a huge difference to this business. Systems have the advantage of eliminating the human factor from much of the running of a business. You see, by having them in place, it's these tried and tested systems that actually run the company. People run the systems. That way you avoid all the nasty and potentially damaging human factors that can often derail even the best intentions.

Luckily for Angeline, she now has a means of choosing the right people as members of her team. You see, systems help her look for the right qualities in a person – one's that fit with her business and those that work there. They make sure she assesses applicants for their enthusiasm, attitude and passion as well as technical skills or other business related factors.

Back to Angeline:

"I need to find another staff member fairly quickly. Then I'll start playing around with some of the things that Steve and I have been talking about. There's a lot of stuff that we've talked about, but haven't yet implemented; just little things like putting up more signage. We can do that quite quickly, and I think it will make quite a difference.

"We've got welcome packs that we're using now. We've just installed a new software package and that is fantastic. When a client arrives, we let it be known that the room had been specially put together for them – with maybe a drink of water and a sweet, or something like that – just little touches that make a big difference.

In 12 months time, the business will look quite different to what it does now, because I've put together a whole lot of different roles that need to be filled. So by having other staff members taking on those roles, it means it doesn't all lie with me; but it doesn't all lie with one other person either. It means that everybody has his or her part to play. For example, we've put together a different training program so a new team member would actually go around and spend a day with the different people who'd actually teach them those things. It means, too, that if that person leaves, I can fill that role quite easily without it being too much of a problem. For example, when I teach a new staff member, I have to go through all the different treatments that we provide. So I've put together a manual.

"There have been lots of things that I've done in that area and obviously that frees up my time and my mind.

"It means that the business is now a lot more stable – not dependant on me or any one person – and this makes me feel good. It means that everybody feels important too. They've got something that they have to do and they know they have to do it well.

"I'd quite like to have a few different businesses without actually having to be there all the time. This is what they talk about, isn't it?

"I want my current business to run on its own, and I'm working towards that. I want to make it really interesting, having really good things for clients so that they're not losing interest, so that we are the only place they'll want to come to. And I think too, that will allow me to get a better class of clientele.

Beauty Therapist Survives Staff Walkout And Prospers

"I don't necessarily want to be so busy that we're all run off our feet. I want clients who we look after, and who appreciate that. I'd rather have quality than quantity …

"Steve has helped me feel more confident … and everyone has commented on the fact that I handled all the changes amazingly well. I'm so much closer to my goals than most people I know. I am working towards that and I have a plan. I'm learning how to implement all of this. I think it will all look very different in the end. And I think people will enjoy their roles, as opposed to feeling like … well, most beauty therapists I know work long hours and sort of feel that they don't get a lot of rewards. I'd like to change that – for myself, for us. For me and my girls."

▮ Building Inspectors Now Have Solid Foundation For Expansion

---

You generally hear that what a man doesn't know doesn't hurt him, but in business what a man doesn't know does hurt.

~ E. St. Elmo Lewis ~

The Business

Name: RealSure Ltd – The House Inspectors

Address: 61 Elmsmere Road, Silverstream, Wellington, New Zealand

Owners: Bruce and Sarah Symon

Type Of Business: Building inspections

Business Sector: House inspections

Started: 2000

Coach: Steve McDonald

The Challenge

One of the great benefits of having a Business Coach is that it gives the owners some form of accountability – it makes them answerable to someone. Yes, I know most business owners say they're answerable to themselves, but I'm talking about someone who ensures they do what they say they will do and when they say it'll be done. I'm talking about someone who motivates, excites and leads business owners to meet their true potential – someone who keeps them focused on the important issues that need to be addressed, in order to achieve whatever goals they've set for themselves.

You see, sometimes the owner doesn't even realise the business can do far better than it is. I mean, everyone always has high hopes and dreams of doing far better than they actually are, but they somehow know deep down that it will never be.

And you know what? They're probably right, because they then have a self-fulfilling prophecy. And there's another thing that ensures they'll never do significantly better than they're doing – they don't know what they don't know.

Bring in a Business Coach and suddenly anything is possible. Suddenly there will be a new perspective on an old challenge. Suddenly there will be momentum, and a new path to follow.

Let's look at a real example. The company is RealSure Ltd, and they're in the Land of the Long White Cloud.

Sarah's Story

Our company is RealSure Ltd. We carry out building inspections on residential properties. Our head office is based out in the Hutt Valley, and we cover the whole Wellington region and the southern point of the Wairarapa.

Our average client is anyone that's buying or selling a property; they tend to be more in the 30-45 age bracket than any other.

We aren't as well known as we'd like to be, because our marketing has been limited due to budget constraints. Our growth is predominantly through word of mouth and we do seem to have a very, very good reputation out there, which is brilliant.

We did do a lot of research when the company was launched and worked with a very good brand marketing company that used to be called Frameworks and are now called Brand New.

We set up expectations for the company's culture, image and desired perception and that all came to be. It did prove that when you plan these things, and take the time to do the research and development, it actually happens. You visualise and it becomes – very much so. We set out to achieve an expectation and perception and we're getting there.

We exceeded our business plan in our first year in business by about 75%, and we're looking at 100% more this year. The growth's been phenomenal. Our plans need to be updated!

The Moment of Truth

The big thing for us was that we had become so entrenched in working IN the business and we knew we needed to work on it. We knew we needed to do something different, so we could allocate the time and continue working on the business to develop it further. We'd reached a certain point where yes, we'd met the plan – the year plan: yes, we'd proven the model; yes, it was a service that's needed;

and yes, we'd achieved all we'd wanted to achieve. Now we had to take it further, and that's where we were at.

Then, probably a couple of months into the new financial year and the new year for our business planning, we realised that we needed to get some help to take us further. We knew what we needed to do; however, we just couldn't seem to make the time. We wanted someone who would have the experience and the knowledge to assist us.

We had a phone system put in and the woman that we were dealing with recommended a web-site designer. The web-site designer had a business that was in the same sort of position that ours was in, and he put us on to Steve … word of mouth!

Firstly, Steve ensured that we put some things down on paper, so we could get back into working to a plan again. And then from there, what we're finding through working with him is that we're actually working through all the things that we need to work through, bit-by-bit. This is happening, because time's allocated, we sit down and discuss what we've done, what we need to do, and we put those goals and plans into place and it happens the next week. So it actually means that we're working through all the business that we need to work through, while working IN the business.

Steve keeps us ON it and IN it, and that's been the fun part.

Our main challenge is that there are not enough hours in the day! So how do we overcome this?

Time is one of the challenges, but it just happens, because as we've set those things in place, when we compile our Weekly Goal Sheet, we know they have to be done. In the spare moments we just go back to the goal sheets and do it, whereas before, it wouldn't have happened.

As for our achievements, we're now moving on again and that's critical. We've had huge growth in our customer base, and because this growth is predominantly word of mouth, that's exponential.

We now have more staff, which relieves us of some of the pressure, which in turn will ensure we can meet demands.

The Coach's Story

When I was approached, the reality was that the business was successful in that it generated great revenues, but its profitability was poor. It also demanded the attendance and all the attention of the owners.

There was a strong desire to make the business operate without them, but no actual strategies to achieve this were yet in place.

The business' ideal goals were:

• To establish a franchise format and to take the business nationally within 12 months.

• To make the business capable of working without the owners.

• To provide an asset base.

• To teach the process of making a successful business operate independent of the owners.

So, where did we start? We started by testing and measuring everything. Every dollar spent on marketing is assessed both before and after the event. We now have a budget and can track the effects of our marketing spend.

We employed a dicta-typist to relieve the pressure on the owners and are currently employing additional team members in the field positions. That is starting to allow the owners to plan and prioritise better. They are now thinking more about business development, planning the growth of the business and looking at the various product and service packages. By enhancing and updating the customer database, they are getting ready to set up and use a customer communication strategy that is designed to develop repeat business, referrals and customer loyalty. Because they have started to think outside the square, they are much more able to respond to rapidly changing circumstances in their industry. They have also been able to test and measure new services as a response to changing demand in the market. When the measurement shows that the market is not responding as anticipated, they are now ready, willing and able to rapidly drop the strategy rather than to continue flogging the 'dead horse'.

The Outcome

Being able to 'steer' people in the right direction by showing them how to take care of the fundamentals of their business in such a way that they don't feel they're being 'told' what to do is the key to achieving sustainable results.

It's also the way to gain their trust and confidence.

"We're on a 12-month goal," says Sarah. "We will have achieved the goals that we have set out to achieve. We will also be in a position where Steve's taught us what we need to know, so we can go solo. Part of his plan is that he's only there for those 12 months, and it's during that time that he'll teach us what we need to know."

It's also important that the coach can communicate with clients. Really communicate. They must talk the same language.

"He's actually really, really brilliant, because what he does is challenge us to think more," continues Sarah. "We are thinking the right way, however, he puts it into business terminology so we actually realise what it is we're doing in textbook terms. This is really nice, as it sort of empowers us in itself, and reassures us that we do know what we're doing.

"The fact that Steve earned Bruce's (co-owner of the business) confidence as well is huge, and that's actually quite a feat for someone. He proved that he could do what we needed him to do and he did it in such a way that he wasn't telling us what to do; he was teaching us how to achieve the things we wanted to achieve, so it's really, really awesome.

"We didn't want someone coming in and telling us what to do – that wasn't necessary as such. But he's giving us another dimension – almost like a sounding board – as well as being a teacher. So it's really very valuable. I'd definitely recommend it to the right person. You've got to have the right attitude for it to work. I can say that because I've done coaching before, and basically it wasn't the right thing for me then. So we were straight up with him on day 1. You know, he really impressed us. He's very genuine; he's not trying to hard sell anything.

"If he tried to convert us we wouldn't have been here, we really wouldn't have. There's too much of that going on and that's inside out thinking, as opposed to outside in. He just quietly showed us how he could help us. Well, we said what we needed, he said how he could assist and showed evidence that he could do that.

"Nike hit it with their slogan – 'Just do it', but know what you're doing! They should have said, 'just do it, but with a bit of forethought!'

"Steve's become quite a valuable member of our team and we value his input."

▮ Kitchen Design Business Experiences A Change Of Heart – And A Change Of Fortune

---

The five essential entrepreneurial skills for success: Concentration, Discrimination, Organization, Innovation and Communication

~ Michael E. Gerber ~

The Business

Name: DK Design Kitchens

Address: 20 Waine Street, Harbord, 2096, NSW, Australia.

Owners: Preben Lemming and Jakob Gamborg

Type Of Business: Kitchen design, sales and manufacturing

Business Sector: Manufacturing

Started: 1995

Coach: Greg Albert

The Challenge

If you've ever lived on a busy road, you'll know that after a while you become oblivious to all the noise – you become immune to the very things that other people find most irritating, frustrating and off-putting. You'll find you begin focusing on other factors; things like convenience, atmosphere and lifestyle as a means of justifying, in your own mind at any rate, why it is you've chosen to live there.

You'll be looking for reasons to stay there, whereas others would be looking for reason why not to stay there. They'll sight factors such as noise, lack of privacy, inconvenience with parking and lack of privacy as good reasons for finding a quieter place to live.

Familiar with the scenario? Good. Then you'll understand that the same can happen in business.

Just because the business owner is engrossed in the job doesn't mean other members of the family are. The spouse could be more than frustrated by the long hours worked and lack of social activity, whereas the owner might see things quite differently. And not as objectively.

Take the case of DK Design Kitchens, for example. The business had grown steadily since its inception, but this was more a result of doing things as they came along than good planning – of luck and lots of hard work.

Both Jakob Gamborg and Preben Lemming had been in the industry before they joined forces. Jakob had been in Sales and Design and Preben in manufacturing. They both felt they could do better than the companies they worked for. You know the story – 'I thought I worked for an idiot BEFORE I went into business for myself.' And if you've read Michael Gerber's book *The E-Myth Revisited*, you'll know what I mean when I say Jakob and Preben were typical technicians. Their only concern in those early days was survival and making enough money to cover expenses.

DK Design Kitchens grew into a design, sales and manufacturing company located on the Northern Beaches of Sydney, with a mission to become the North Shore's most prestigious joinery business.

Preben is in charge of production while Jakob is in charge of sales and design. Preben's wife Pernille looks after administration and accounts.

Everything seemed to be ticking over nicely – or was it?

Pernille's Story

We first came to hear about *ACTION International* when we were offered a free business diagnostic through a direct mail letter. We took up the offer and found out how much more *ACTION International* could do for us, although we still weren't sure anyone from outside could help our company.

At the time of meeting Greg Albert from *ACTION*, the company had grown to 15 employees. Our sales were OK – though not great – but workflow and speed in the factory was in disarray. It is safe to say our team was not happy, and we had a lot of 'reworks' and some unhappy customers.

When Jakob first met Greg, he said, "This guy can't tell me anything about selling and sales; I have been doing this for 12 years and know what to do." However, I knew something had to change; we were working long hours, not making much profit and had a lot of fires to put out.

Preben thought nothing would help the guys in the workshop. "They are all hopeless and you can't teach them anything," he said. "They just don't care."

He also knew he couldn't carry on with things the way they were.

Greg came and had a talk to us, and everyone thought it would be a good thing to sign up. We agreed Greg should come and do an Alignment Report for us. This turned out to be very healthy, as it made us think about the future. In truth, I really pushed for it, as I knew Preben and Jakob needed to do things differently.

Anyway, we didn't sign up with **ACTION** straight away since it was just before Christmas and everyone was very busy, and probably a bit scared, to commit.

The Moment Of Truth

It all came to a head just days before Christmas. Preben had some really bad days with 'the boys' and came to Jakob and said, "I've had enough. I can't take it anymore!"

My first thought was to call Greg Albert and talk to him about what we could do to turn Preben around to being happy again.

That was when we signed up with **ACTION** and started our coaching program with Greg Albert.

One of the first things Greg asked us to do was to read **The E-Myth Revisited**, which taught us how, in every business, there is a technician, an entrepreneur and a manager. It showed us how the different types of people look at things differently.

We also found out who was who in our business. Jakob is the entrepreneur who looks to the future, Preben is the technician who looks at today and

I am the manager who looks at the past.

Greg then asked us what our weekly/monthly sales were. We really couldn't tell him. Any Key Performance Indicators that he asked for, we also couldn't supply. It was a real awakening for us all. We then knew what we needed to do, but had no idea how we would get the time to do it.

Greg suggested we produce a Procedures Manual.

As we didn't have a mission statement, vision statement or culture in place, or even an organizational chart, we clearly had a lot to do. It took us quite a while to get through some of the ideas and suggestions that Greg gave us. Slowly it all came together. Greg was very patient, but kept pushing us forward. It got to the point where we really looked forward to the coaching calls. When we began to have the figures we needed, it was very easy to move forward. We also uncovered a lot of things that needed tightening.

The Coach's Story

DK Design Kitchens was an unusual case for me, in so far as I was approached by one of the owners' wives (Pernille), and not the owner himself (Preben). This was out of utter frustration with her husband, whom she knew needed help, as business was overwhelming them.

To compound matters, the business was a partnership and it was not the dominant owner's wife who contacted me.

So both owners were NOT on board when coaching began.

The one owner (Preben) decided to give it a go, as nothing else was working. Jakob just said OK and went along with it. It was obvious from day 1 that both were not in alignment and Jakob was not on board.

I actually felt like walking away from this situation, however, Pernille virtually begged me not to.

I then took a stand as a Coach and stepped up.

I demanded to call a 4-hour manager's team meeting at which I would present. My attitude was I would either 'crash or burn' there. I spent time talking about the psychology of success in people and business. I was really talking to Jakob, hoping he would get it. It was very intense.

Well, he did. He rang me two days later and said, "OK, I get it. I need to change. I am ready." The coaching was on course from that point on.

The situation was that the business was running, yet the major items like culture, the team, or going the extra mile were not happening. This is where I spent most of the early time – basically getting Jakob and Preben to become real leaders by inspiring people to follow, rather than just telling them what to do!

We spent time developing all the SPIRITUAL points of the business first – Culture, Vision, Mission, Rules, etc. We then re-launched the company to the Team.

Once this had taken place, we worked on the development of the sales team and the marketing activities. I must say, I cannot recall anything that really did not work, as by now Testing & Measuring was a culture, embedded into the way things were done. We tried different techniques and methods until they worked.

One thing that was interesting was we came up with a slogan 'Dare To Be Different'. We tried an advertisement that went against all advertising principles – it was a plain white rectangle with 'Dare To Be Different' in the middle.

The company's name, in very small lettering, was at bottom. THAT WAS ALL. You can imagine how weird this looked in amongst all the normal kitchen ads that contained offers and pictures. It worked! Not only did the leads increase, but we received a higher level of client. Their target market now was $15,000+ kitchens.

Once this was all working efficiently, we put Key Performance Indicators (KPI's) and management tools in place, and spent a long time on the financial management side of the business. Soon we had spreadsheets and graphs for everything from Cashflow and Sales, to Conversion and Factory Efficiency. This really gave them a sense of understanding and control of their business.

The Outcome

By having systems and reporting KPI's in place, DK Design Kitchens now have a solid business, so much so that they are purchasing their own purpose-built facilities and moving out of their rented premises to start their next growth phase.

"Our biggest achievement was working out the new price list, and changing the commission structure and quotation method," Pernille says. "We lost some sales staff and took on new ones, and we now have better profit than ever. Greg really has us focused on profit, not turnover. As a result, we were suddenly making more profit with a lot less effort."

Getting the rest of the team involved was the next challenge.

"We had Greg give the team training and motivation to keep them focused, and we put KPI's in place for them too. We even had Greg re-launch the company at our Christmas function. He introduced our new vision, mission, culture and rules of the game to the rest of the team. We really started to get results with less headaches and business was fun again."

Having fun at work is so important, yet not many people realise that.

"Our aim was to get rid of the 'bad fruit' among the team and to get new, more productive personnel. We did this by letting them de-select themselves from our new culture and rules. There are, of course, still procedures which haven't been written down, but the company is running a lot smoother than before we met Greg Albert."

People are, of course, an important dynamic in any business. They come and go, and that's only natural. But when this happens, many businesses aren't able to cope. That's why it's so important to have systems in place.

"Our top salesperson decided to start his own business," continues Pernille. "Before, this would have been a disaster. Now, with systems in place – a great recruitment process and a KPI management system – we were able to not only replace him, but to put others on to grow the business as well."

Preben still looks after production, but now has a foreman who checks, measures and makes cutting lists, and he has also put on his own installers who fit with the culture. Jakob is now running design and sales. He looks after and supports his sales team, and has focused on setting and managing the KPI's.

During the past 12 months, their average dollar sale increased by 40% and they increased their prices by 10%. This resulted in an increase in turnover of 30%, but more significantly their profitability is much healthier. Whereas the business previously ran at a slight loss, DK Design Kitchens has just managed to record a net profit of $250,000. Their turnover was $3 million.

Pernille is still running administration, but due to the rest of the company running smoother, the accounts, cashflow and Profit and Loss functions are now reviewed monthly. Everyone knows their targets.

Pernille reports that they now have a happy team and the climate at 'work' is excellent. "It is fun going to work. We have weekly sales/admin team meetings and the factory have weekly 'wifle' (what I feel like expressing) sessions where team members get together to freely express their feelings. This has helped to weed out all the negative elements, and we now have a pro-active team."

Weekly/Monthly statistics and comparisons are produced and the Salesperson Of The Month is rewarded at the end of every month. Targets are set and closely monitored.

"We now feel we are in control of the business, and not the other way round. There is always a smile on the faces of Preben and Jakob and the 'lows' are becoming more and more rare. You can feel the buzz in the air and this rubs off on our customers. We are now booked months in advance!"

Of course, the company still faces challenges, which they try to solve as they arise. The difference now is that all challenges are analysed and understood so they don't occur again.

"But as everyone knows, in small business everything has its ups and downs. We just tackle the challenges in a different way to what we did before," continues Pernille. "We now look for solutions and how we can add a system of our own.

Incredibly, we have just purchased our own new factory, office and showroom and are going to set it all up for perfect production and workflow. In fact, we will set it up now with everything we learnt from Greg and *ACTION*. We are all very exited about what we have achieved and what we have today. We look forward to the future, and thank the day we called Greg and asked for help that fateful Christmas, when we basically had had enough!"

▌ Smallest Retail Outlet Becomes Number 3 Performer For National Franchise Group

Above all, we wish to avoid having a dissatisfied customer. We consider our customers a part of our organization, and we want them to feel free to make any criticism they see fit in regard to our merchandise or service. Sell practical, tested merchandise at reasonable profit, treat your customers like human beings — and they will always come back.

~ L.L. Bean ~

The Business

Name: Harvey Norman Computer Store

Address: Maitland, New South Wales, Australia

Owner: Glen Gregory

Type Of Business: Computer retailer

Business Sector: Retail

Started: 1999

Coach: Graham Dunkley

The Challenge

There are basically three ways of getting into business – you can start one yourself, you can buy one wholesale or you can buy retail. But remember, buying retail means you're paying the retail price, which includes an element of profit. And, although I usually recommend you never pay the retail price for a business, there are instances when it's advisable. One of these is when it's a franchise you're buying into.

You see, if you're buying a proven franchise, many of the pitfalls will already have been removed, and you'll generally be able to hit the ground running. Going the franchise route often enables you to fast track both your profits as well as your learning experience. Yet the fact remains, entering business this way is no bed of roses. You still need to call on all your entrepreneurial skills if you really want to thrive.

Take Glen Gregory, for instance. Glen was the franchisee of Harvey Norman Computer Store in Maitland, New South Wales. This store had been operating for some 8 or 9 years, with two previous owners and a change of location 3 years before Graham was taken on as coach.

The store is part of a Harvey Norman complex with Electrical and Furniture in the same building. They all share a common entrance.

Always a profitable outlet, it boasted the smallest selling area of all the Group's outlets. Space was at a premium. The staff were mostly untrained and had indifferent sales experience gained only from a wide range of previous employers. Only a few had a strong background in computer-related fields.

None of them, and that includes Glen, had any concept of a consistent, scripted sales process, repeated follow-up, the high-level of service necessary to create raving fans with a long lifetime relationship, or of giving the store the 'wow' factor.

Until they took on a Business Coach, that is.

Glen's Story

To better understand Glen's story, it would help to understand, in broad terms, the way people behave. One system I recommend is the DISC Personality Profile, which was designed by the American Psychologist Dr. William Moulton Marsden back in the 1920's. It places people into one of four different personality types, or categories; D – Dominant, I – Influential, S – Steady or C – Compliant.

It is an accurate personality analysis that can be used to predict the behaviour of individuals when they work on their own and with others.

According to the DISC Personality Profile, Glen is a High D. High D's like to be in control. They want to be at the top and give the orders. They have a hard time following orders, as they feel their own way is always better. High D's will usually end up in managing positions, self-employed or in charge of a section that has a bit of room to move unsupervised.

They like to be in control of their own lives and make their own decisions. High D's can seem to be too powerful or too strong for other people. They are confident, outspoken, and say what they feel. This can offend others, as they can be thought of as arrogant. They aren't usually; it's just the way they express themselves.

As High D's have active minds that like to be stimulated, they like to be doing lots of things at once. When they do more than one thing at a time, the quality can start to drop. It can be difficult for them to follow something to its end. They feel a great need for lots of activity. When you want something done in a hurry, give it to a High D.

Now back to Glen.

Glen had a hard, competitive youth, which drove his high-D personality style, a natural instinct for business, a good reputation in the Harvey Norman Group and a burning desire to do what Gerry Harvey (the Group's founder) had done! But his teen years had been unkind, and he had few assets to help get him there.

"Having the opportunity to be a Harvey Norman Franchisee is like waking up to dream every morning," says Glen. "Gerry Harvey asks you to take up a franchise, for which you get to build your own empire. All proprietors want to be No. 1, yet we all want to work together and help each other to make Harvey Norman the No. 1 Retail Company in Australia and the world."

The Moment of Truth

Glen never really experienced a moment of truth – or something that told him he needed help. Far from it. He was a young gun who knew he was good and thought he knew it all.

"I was achieving very good results within my first 2 franchises, with little experience or qualification, but I wanted to be better. I wanted to be No 1. I knew I had to widen my vision and knowledge in order to understand retail better – so I could sell more and make more," continues Glen.

"As luck would have it, one of my staff and his father were Business Coaches and to me this sounded like what I needed to improve myself, yet I was sceptical as to how much it would help. But I was committed to continually improving my store and myself."

Graham talked him into taking on coaching. However, he later confessed that he was extremely skeptical at first …. he could not see what a professional pharmacist could know, or for that matter, teach him about information technology or computer sales!

So, almost as a favour, he reluctantly agreed to Graham's proposition. "Hell, what did I have to lose?" laughs Glen. "If this guy was any good at all, I might learn a few things and where would be the harm in that?"

Graham started talking about living above the line, about testing and measuring, and leadership … and he made Glen read books!

Glen hated reading! But he got down to it and read motivational books and watched videos. He read about the myths we all believe, about entrepreneurs, how we get into business and why we often end up hating what we once loved doing. He learnt why, when we run out of ideas, we just keep doing the same things, which makes us quietly go crazy. And he read books about success.

"Graham promised that I would be able to achieve greater results, but it would all be up to me. I had to put the hard work in, and Graham would give me the tools to grow the business."

Graham then talked him into putting his entire team through a one-day sales course. Needless to say this included him too! The penny had dropped. They realised they could do other things besides discounting!

The team came back all fired up.

Glen then had his coach put them through team training, and once again he included himself in that team. He suddenly realised that anyone can manage, but it takes skill to be a leader and to communicate well.

He began learning all about leverage in business.

Glen and his team were taught that all the national advertising in the world only gets the prospect to the door. What the team does from that moment on, to make it a memorable buying experience, is what explodes a business and takes them all to the top.

They learned that treating their clients with honour, respect, warmth and empathy creates a long-term trusting relationship, which then spawns greater opportunities for profitable sales than all the incessant give-aways that traditionally feature in TV advertising.

Suddenly their conversion rate, transaction rate and profitability climbed, and best of all, this great new team started having fun!

"Over the course of 12 months, with Graham as my mentor, I was able to learn the values of a team and how to use it to greater effect. I began to understand the business cycle where Boss looks after Staff, Staff look after Customers, Customers look after the Business, and the Business looks after the Boss. Simple, but solid," enthuses Glen.

"Watching *ACTION'S* video seminars, reading some suggested books, studying direct marketing methods, feeding and bouncing ideas off Graham - every week I was learning something new. I began looking at my business in a different way."

Coach's Comment

Glen, always a good manager, quickly became one of the Harvey Norman Group's star franchisees and his team came to be acknowledged as something special by the industry's account managers. Such was the store's performance that the national executive chose Glen to take on a fairly young and under-performing store in the northern suburbs of Perth.

So, 8 months later, Glen and I parted company, the task at Maitland left unfinished. Maitland's loss was to be Perth's great gain – Glen's new store became one of the State's top 3 performers within 18 months.

Glen became so magnetic as a manager and leader that it wasn't long before 3 of the Maitland team joined him in Perth.

The Outcome

From a reluctant, even cynical beginning, Glen was hungry for new ideas and was able to apply them quickly. He conquered his shortcomings as a leader and communicator, rapidly gaining the wisdom to understand other personalities in his team and to get the best from them.

In only 8 months, he grew his turnover by nearly 18%, from $9.2 million to over $11 million, and raised the profit from 10.1% to nearly 17%. His average unit sale climbed 16% to around $193. His annual client transaction rate rose by nearly 7%. And what's more he achieved this during what is widely regarded as the poorest period in recent memory for computer sales across the nation, when many retailers were recording negative growth.

His team's efforts, spurred on by his infectious enthusiasm, made the Maitland store (which you might remember, had the smallest floor space of any Harvey Norman computer outlet) number 3 in profitability for the entire Group.

This is a great result by any standards. And even though Glen was working within a well-established franchise operation, having an independent, objective mentor paid off handsomely.

"As Harvey Norman franchisees, when we are looking at how to improve something within our business, we usually look at another Harvey Norman stores or even at our competition. With *ACTION International* being involved with thousands of companies, I found working with Graham enabled me to draw on companies that were in different industries, yet had great ideas that could be applied to my store," explains Glen.

"Without doubt, my 12 months with Graham strengthened my ability to be the No. 1 Franchisee within Harvey Norman. My team at the Maitland store was exactly that, a TEAM. The whole team wanted to be No 1. We all wanted to make a higher gross profit. We all wanted to sell more. We all wanted to provide the highest level of customer service possible. The whole team was involved in training and enjoyed the challenge of improving ourselves."

Even though Glen was a really good businessman before he took on a Coach, that didn't prevent him from reaching new levels of excellence.

"I was achieving good results before *ACTION International*, but I wasn't content with how much I really knew and wanted to step-up a few levels. Today, I am a better Harvey Norman Proprietor and a better businessman. I believe within Harvey Norman we all could be better businessmen."

▌ From Failure To Franchising In No Time At All

Method goes far to prevent trouble in business: for it makes the task easy, hinders confusion, saves abundance of time, and instructs those that have business depending, both what to do and what to hope.

~ William Penn ~

The Business

Name: The CHAD Group, Inc.

Address: PO Box 224 Lititz, PA 17543, USA

Owner: Chad Longenecker

Type Of Business: Computer retailer

Business Sector: Residential builder/remodeler

Started: 1999

Coach: Eric Dombach

The Challenge

The range of challenges faced by small business owners is as diverse as there are businesses, and we've looked at quite a few in this book already. Most have certain external factors hindering their progress, and this, as we've seen, is fairly typical.

But how about the case where the problem lies internally, so to speak? I'm thinking here about cases where the external factors are all favourable, yet the business still seems to be struggling.

I came across a great example in America recently. Let me explain ...

The CHAD Group of Lancaster, PA had been in existence for 2 years when they realised they weren't making any progress at all towards achieving their business goal of being one of the best, and most profitable, builders and remodellers in their area. In fact, even though their local area was fairly affluent, and the local economy was in great shape, they were finding it hard to make headway. The business environment was more than favourable too – it was ideally suited to a business such as theirs. The population consisted of a good mix of people who had grown up there and those who had moved in due to the area's growth and good economy. They were predominantly upper-middle class folk who had a good outlook on life and lived in pockets of tightly-knit communities throughout the county.

Furthermore, Chad says his business was well accepted by the community, even though there was lots of competition in the marketplace. In fact, he says there was more than enough business for everyone.

So, what was the problem?

OK, I have to be honest; things aren't always so straightforward in business. There were a few external negative factors they were up against, but viewed against the good economy and favourable local situation, they weren't major inhibiting factors. I'm talking here about the almost universal stereotype of the construction industry – you know, always being over budget, not keeping the site clean and never being on time. But this was a level playing field – these external factors affected all the players equally.

"Being a new business, we had a lot of debt," explains Chad. "We desperately needed to develop cashflow, as we were losing money every day. We also needed to increase our number of leads and I needed to improve my ability to close deals. And I also needed a system to regulate my customer service and quality."

Chad shared some challenges with his competitors, like finding reliable workers with a good work ethic and who truly cared about the customer. But this alone wouldn't have accounted for his poor business performance.

In a nutshell, the business was heading towards certain failure.

Chad's Story

I'm just your average American guy. I spend my leisure time playing golf, doing home improvements, watching football and gymnastic events with my wife Tracy, vacationing on Florida beaches and playing with my children Catelin and Chase.

I'd like to achieve financial security, have fun and enjoy life. I'd like to raise my children into great adults and I'd like to have a great family life. I'd also like to work less than 40 hours a week, so I can volunteer my time mentoring under-privileged kids.

Tracy, too, would like to have financial security and the ability to volunteer her time. She would like not to have to work full-time.

I see myself achieving these goals through building a successful, profitable business that can eventually run without me. That would enable us to retire early and to travel around the world. I'd like to be able to draw a passive income from my business, which will one day include divisions focused on remodelling, new homes, property management, and light to heavy commercial and restoration work.

I went into business originally because I wanted more opportunity than I was getting working for my father. I wanted to build a track record of satisfied customers and a strong referral base for my business – and a strong cashflow. So far I have achieved the first, and am working on the second.

My immediate goal is to become more profitable. I'd also like to learn to delegate responsibility so that I can work less in the field and more on building the business. I'd like to provide a great work environment for my team and I'd like to achieve $700,000 in sales this year – this would take just 1 more house and a few more remodelling jobs.

I'm presently working 50 or 60 hours each week – my aim is to cut that down to 40 within the next 2 or 3 years. And I'd like to take home $100,000 a year, so Tracy can quit working. This is triple my present income.

My other main goals include creating a business that runs like a well-oiled machine, and developing systems to turn around estimates faster, to create job schedules, to keep team members motivated and working hard, to follow-up on jobs consistently and to maintain a high-quality customer service. And I'd like to achieve $2-million in sales next year.

The Moment Of Truth

I was invited to play Leverage, Brad Sugars' board game, one evening and it was there that I met Eric. He set up a meeting and demonstrated the power of the *ACTION* Coaching Program. We then scheduled a second meeting to include my wife, and a couple of days later we decided to go ahead with coaching. This was a very difficult decision for us to make as we were losing money at the time. But I just knew I desperately needed the education – and someone to be accountable to.

Coach's Comment

I began testing and measuring Chad's lead sources. We put in place about 10 new lead generation campaigns and a handful of them began working and bringing in new leads. We also began working on formalising a sales process. I worked hard on improving Chad's salesmanship, getting him to read books on sales, and doing sales role-plays with his wife, myself and another *ACTION* Coach. We developed an extensive selling system that included various things to deliver Raving Fans quality service during the sales process. Since then his conversion rate has improved from 11% to 41% on the jobs he's been bidding for.

The plan was to firstly concentrate hard on increasing sales, followed by conversion rate strategies.

Chad cut costs by moving out of his office and into a home office and letting go of his secretary until the cashflow improves markedly.

We then began testing and measuring everything. We measured advertising and return on investment, leads, conversion percentage, average dollar sale, number of transactions, and monthly breakeven numbers.

The business has made significant strides in its conversion rate, as well as in testing and measuring. They have found new and effective lead generation strategies that include strategic alliances with restoration contractors and other general contractors. Chad joined a networking group, which has resulted in lots of new leads. We also implemented a referral program to encourage referrals.

Significant changes were made to the business owner's routine. He now has someone he is accountable to, he has deadlines by which to implement new ideas, and he is forced to do things that he knows he has to do, but could never quite make the time to do before.

The Outcome

Chad is now working his way out of debt and the future looks bright.

"I think we are doing the right things to turn things around and to make an incredible success story," Chad says. "We're now landing a lot of really nice jobs. I have a total of 4 team members in the field and I'm running the office myself. We've worked extensively on putting great systems in place to make sure that our customers get 1st class service and are treated like kings and queens by each of our team members."

The business has some very powerful strengths that it is working on; these include innovation and creativity in design and construction. They excel in taking people's challenging conceptual ideas and turning them into reality. They are working very hard on communicating with their customers more efficiently. They want to ensure their customers take decisions fast enough to keep their construction process moving. They also want to improve the turn around time on estimates and to improve productivity in the field. And they want to develop a sense of teamwork. They realise that by greatly increasing sales they will over stress their internal support structures.

"When the business is in a strong, healthy cashflow position, I'd like to franchise it, because the systems we've created are so good," says Chad. "If it was hard for me to get this business started, then I know it's hard for lots of other guys to get a remodelling business started."

Chad has come a long way since taking on a Business Coach. He started out by being burdened with a horrible cashflow and creditors crying out to be paid. This was overcome by setting up payment plans with them, getting a new accountant, watching business ratios to spot trends, and testing and measuring lead sources and conversion rates.

"Before working with *ACTION International*, we hardly measured anything. Now Eric has us testing and measuring just about everything. Because of the systems he helped us put in place, I can now tell you exactly how many leads we need each month to break even for the month, and how much profit I will make for each additional lead. We've also made significant improvements in our sales process and customer guarantees. We've added a referral program and joined a referral based networking group. After working with Eric, our conversion rate has tripled from 11% to a whopping 41%. Now, I never feel like I am wasting my time when I do an estimate. It's very exiting to know that for every 3 estimates I do I'll get one job. With Eric's guidance we continue to improve each and every week. I now have a much more positive outlook on the future of my company. Thanks Eric!"

▌ Security Products Manufacturer No Longer Confined By Mediocre Performance

---

*Learning is not compulsory
but neither is survival.*

~ *W. Edwards Deming* ~

The Business

Name: Taplin Security Products

Address: 95 Toombul Road, Northgate, Queensland, Australia.

Owners: Bill and Pam Ruddle (and son Bill Jnr)

Type Of Business: Security barrier manufacturers and retailers

Business Sector: Manufacturing

Purchased: 1990

Coach: David Enright

The Challenge

As I mentioned at the beginning of this book, business owners these days tend to spend far too much time working IN their business rather than ON it. But if they want to really produce spectacular results, this has to change. This basic problem has got to be the single biggest impediment to success I've come across in all the thousands of companies I've worked with.

And it's not something that only the most basic owner-operators do – it's common practice across the board. Even those who have a detailed understanding or working experience of business principles do it. They find themselves operating at the specialist level rather than concentrating on becoming a generalist.

Take Bill Ruddle of Taplin Security Products, for example. Before he bought his business, he had extensive corporate experience that included Australian College of

Management training, so he could be forgiven for thinking he was well equipped for running his own show. Believe me – he's not alone. To his credit, though, he had the foresight to recognise the signs and take on a Business Coach.

So, what was the nature of the problem that led him to seek outside professional assistance?

Bill's original goal was to increase turnover by 100%. He recognised the need to work more on, rather than in, the business, and desired to make a minimum of $100,000 profit, to take a holiday, improve product quality, to be the best in customer service, and to allow Pam to retire. Nothing wrong with that.

So what happened?

The Ruddles quickly lost sight of where they were heading and how they were going to get there. They became bogged down in the day-to-day routine of running the business and became enslaved by outmoded industry cultures and entrenched ways of operating.

Bill's Story

After running the business for 11 years, things were getting better but we'd only had a 100% increase in 10 years – that's only about 7-8% per year growth. We were marking time and wondering if we'd be able to reach our retirement goals. We were actually running at a Net Loss. The GST had really impinged on cashflow. Morale was very low, and we felt we were at the mercy of our subcontractors as we relied on them for the manufacture and installation of our products.

We actually didn't know how we could improve the business, other than just putting our heads down and working harder. In fact, I think it's fair to say that we didn't even know if our business was improvable! I mean, it had been in existence since 1955 and when we bought it, we simply continued doing what had been done all along. We thought our performance was normal for the type of business we were in, even though we would have liked better results.

We were worried that it was looking more and more like we would fall far short of our long-term retirement goals, but then again, that's what most people feel, isn't it?

The Moment Of Truth

I guess our Moment Of Truth arrived by way of a single phone call out of the blue. It was from **ACTION International** and it forced me to face up to my worst business fears. Or the reality of my situation. It made me confront reality, even though my initial reaction was to dismiss it by treating it like just another unsolicited piece of speculative marketing. I retrospect I have to say that this one phone call really changed our lives.

Coach's Comment

It all started after I had posted them a direct mail piece, and when my telemarketer followed it up with a phone call, Bill was very gruff and curt and asked us to stop wasting his time. I immediately got on the phone and assured him that we weren't, and that we probably could add a lot of value to his business if he had any challenges.

We arranged a time to meet and I conducted a Diagnostic of his business. It quickly became evident that Bill was in an uncomfortable situation and was looking for a way out. Sales were stagnant and his structure and relationship with his subcontractors (who he absolutely relied on) was causing him and Pam a lot of worry. There was no Testing and Measuring being done, and the atmosphere in both the office and workshop was tense to say the least. The only form of marketing they were doing was through the Yellow Pages, and Bill was spending his time acting as their salesperson. Cashflow and costs were a major issue due to the subcontractor's high costs.

Bill was keen to commence coaching, but Pam was understandably reluctant to spend the money. Once I was given the go-ahead, I started with the Alignment Consultation to define their real goals and prioritise what challenges needed to be addressed.

The goal was set to increase sales to 30% above their usual budget within 90 days. Education-wise I started by getting them to read Michael Gerber's book, *The E-Myth* and Brad Sugars' book *Instant Cashflow*. They began to see how things could work differently.

The next area I worked on was their sales process and their conversion rate. We also began testing and measuring everything. An organization chart was drawn up showing what the business looked like at the time, and another to detail what it should look like when 'finished'. We introduced scripts and follow-ups to sales. We systemised simple routines and installed a Job Work Flow System, which dramatically increased the ease of processing job orders and the flow of information between sales, the office, the workshop and the client. We also prepared clear budgets and targets.

Things began to move quickly, and it became clear that the existing structure that involved relying on contractors was detrimental to the business' interests. The costs were simply too high and there wasn't sufficient control. However, changing this would prove difficult because it was the way it always was done and relationships and a tight working culture had been established over many years.

That week our normal 1-hour coaching call lasted 2 hours, and proved to be pivotal to unlocking the true potential of the business. Within a few days, the incumbent but troublesome contractor was history, and the Ruddles now had an employee on wages. Whereas the previous contractor had earned approximately

$1,000 for 3 days work, the new employee was now doing a better quality job, 5 days a week, for approximately $500. This proved to be a key turning point for the business in more ways than one. Both Bill and Pam's mindset changed and they began to reassert control over their business, which until then had been controlling them.

Taplin Security's culture began to change for the better.

The next crucial step we took was in the sales area. Bill had been working as the salesperson, and despite being by nature very customer-oriented and excellent at selling the benefits of his product, he suffered from severe self-image limitations. Changing his image was the next crucial factor to his success and it was achieved through perturbation and using Spencer Johnson and Larry Wilson's book, *The One Minute Sales Person*.

The Outcome

After just 3 months the results posted were over budget by some 75%. That was way over the 30% Bill had hoped for and later told me he thought we had 'Buckleys' chance of achieving.

Sales continued to climb largely thanks to the renewed and rejuvenated customer focus. Record sales months were posted and by month 6 Bill was leveraged out of sales and a salesperson recruited. This allowed him to work more on the business instead of in it. Fine-tuning continued for a year, with the end result being that sales were up by 65% over the year and the previous year's Net Loss was turned into a healthy Net Profit.

Recognizing the benefits of the coaching program, Bill and Pam decided to continue on for another 6 months in order to implement further changes. We immediately took measures to fortify the gains made during the first 12 months. As most businesses fail the year after they record their largest growth, we analysed the figures and determined that costings needed refining. 2 of the 3 product sets they stocked were sometimes sold at a loss in a very price competitive market. It was decided that, in future, they would only be sold at full margin with no discounts applicable. Since this decision was taken, both products have been selling well, with no adverse effects whatsoever.

During the next 6-month period, Taplin continued to rewrite its record books and recorded multiple months with sales up 400% on previous average months before coaching commenced, with stronger Net Profit due to cost improvements. They are really beginning to see the compounding effect of the strategies implemented during the first 12 months.

Then, during the 1st week of November 2002, Taplin recorded their highest ever sales week. Sales were almost twice that of a previous average Month! Furthermore, Bill Snr and Bill Jnr took a Friday off to go fishing – a first while he's run the business.

So is he delighted with the results achieved so far?

Absolutely.

"The most notable changes have been so many little things," he says. "Particularly with our attitude and confidence, and now our goals don't seem the insurmountable mountain we always thought they were. Testing and measuring has been a huge success; knowing who our customers are and where they come from, as well as improving our service and consciously making it easy for them to do business with us. Personally, our attitude and confidence in ourselves has changed significantly for the better. The challenge was actually keeping control of the business, especially during times of growth, and not letting it control us."

But their results have been more concrete than that.

"Since starting coaching we've had a 65% increase in sales in the 12 months to the end of June, with an even better profit result. And this has been in a very competitive market that is going through a cyclical downturn with some businesses still closing down."

What lies ahead for the business, now that they've unlocked their true potential?

"This year we plan to grow our turnover to $1M, which will be the same dollar increase we've just been through, and we can refine our profit even more. Also after all this growth, we're looking forward to taking some real time off – a week off soon, and then maybe a fortnight later on in the year. Before coaching, it just wasn't a possibility, but we can really see that happening now. Coaching really got us out of the mud. Before we were in the dark, now we can see."

▌ What Does It Take To Succeed?

*Successful people are successful because
they form the habits of doing those things
that failures don't like to do.*

~ Albert Gray ~

Once upon a time to succeed in business all you had to do was work really hard, put in long hours and be as tenacious as a foxy dog. Back then there was no such thing as the Internet or the global economy, and GST was a term that had even not been coined.

Since then, the business world has matured and small business owners now face a mortality rate high enough to scare them into the thought of going back and getting a job. They have to survive in a world where dropping the ball for a second could mean bankruptcy or even worse.

And yet small business survives … and for a knowledgeable group, it is profitable as well. So what is the secret, how do some businesses bring in super-profits while others work and work and work for nothing? And how do you implement this secret into your business?

The secret is a Business Coach, and all it takes is one phone call.

You've read about some of the amazing success stories businesses all over the world have had through coaching. And it doesn't matter in what country they're in or what size their business is, the results are all quite spectacular. And it also doesn't matter how experienced the businessowner is either. The examples I've written about in this book span as wide a range of businesses as you could imagine. You see, business coaching levels the playing field and gives your business the upper hand. No longer will you need to be your own expert. The advantage comes from having someone to bounce ideas off, someone to teach you how to resolve your own issues, achieve your goals, make you accountable and give you the support you need to stay focused. Suddenly you will have an advisor, when before you only had yourself.

Don't get me wrong, you can survive in business without a Coach, but you will never thrive.

What Does It Take To Succeed?

You see, a Coach will work with you on every area of your business ... sales, marketing and advertising, team building and recruitment, systems and business development, customer service and of course, turnover and profitability. Over a 12-month period, you will be able to relinquish more and more of your day-to-day tasks and take a strategic role in your business - until you reach the point where you actually become the business owner, instead of an employee in your own company. Imagine ... how much difference it will make if you work ON your business, instead of IN it.

But having a Business Coach isn't in itself enough to guarantee your business will fly. There's one other important ingredient, and that's you need to be what I call 'coachable'. You need to be hungry for success and willing to do whatever it takes to get there.

To illustrate what I mean, I asked two of my Business Coaches to talk about the similarities they've found in all the successful people they've coached. I asked them to describe their similarities or things they had in common.

According to Greg Albert, there is a huge difference between extraordinary and ordinary.

"One thing I would like to make clear first, is this," he began. "I come into contact with hundreds of Business Owners and yet only a very small percentage actually decide to seek the assistance of a Business Coach. There are some that could never be coached as their minds are so closed, or so full of fear and scepticism that they will never be outstanding. Others are so focused on saving money that they don't realize that if they don't grow and change, they will never reach the success they desire. These people can become disenchanted, even bitter, or they just run out of the enthusiasm that made them start their own business originally."

Patrick Bright agrees. "I find that the most successful clients I have worked with – no matter what is happening in their life or business – are looking towards the future. Too many people are looking in the rear view mirror and that is why they are having so many accidents and problems. The ones that are looking ahead can see what is coming, and get out of the way or come up with a strategy to overcome the obstacles."

Greg says these people are 'coachable'. "This means they know where they want to go, and realize they need assistance to get there. They are eager to learn and grow and want to be pushed outside their comfort zones. I now regard this as a must when talking to potential clients that seek my assistance. Are you coachable, I ask?"

Patrick puts it this way: "Attitude, the desire to succeed, and a 'do whatever it takes' attitude is a common trait. I have had the greatest success with clients who are willing to do whatever it takes. Unfortunately, they are often in a lot of pain financially or are able to get to a state of high dissatisfaction quickly. The clients I have coached with their backs against the wall produced the greatest results in the shortest amount of time. I think this is because they are prepared to do something there, and then and to take a risk as they have nothing to lose, because if they don't, they soon won't have a business at all."

Greg agrees. "They are willing to take massive action. These people are prepared to do whatever it takes. If something is not working, what can they change to get the result? Most business owners are either too scared or too comfortable to take massive action."

It's all about being decisive.

"People who ask the most questions and don't let their egos get in the way will often admit they don't have all the answers, so they take on new ideas," continued Pat. "They are willing to try new things and new marketing ideas. They are optimistic. They make quick decisions, but whether they're right or wrong isn't the issue; at least they made a decision and learned from it."

Greg says successful people also strive for outstanding results. "Not just good, or better, or OK, but outstanding. So many business owners out there really do not know how simple this is. Just focus on the mediocre service you get in the market today and you will find endless opportunities. People remember really bad and really outstanding people, not the OK's. Ask any Sports Star. Successful people, like Sports Stars, are willing to go the extra mile and want the Coach to push them."

"They truly believe anything is possible," continues Pat. "They don't listen to the word NO. They are persistent. They are prepared to learn from someone who says NO to them. I personally believe I have learnt more from the people who said no to me than from the ones that said yes."

This brings us to another very important characteristic – vision. Greg has found that usually this vision grows as they start to see the results of their hard work pay off. "The best clients I have ever had are the ones who had vision and dreams – and a passion to make it happen. These people don't call them goals; they call them 'musts' because if it is a must, you will surely find a way. As a Coach, these clients give you a whole new set of challenges keeping them on track, but boy it is a whole lot more fun than trying to drag a horse to water!"

Of course, successful people are also great leaders. Both Pat and Greg agree. "They are great leaders, even if at first they are only leading themselves," Pat says. "They must be able to lead a team towards a common goal. They are passionate team builders with clear goals. And they are prepared to take a risk and to have a go."

"With their vision and passion they inspire the team around them to live not only the company's dream, but their own," adds Greg. "They believe in leverage, and the fact that you and your business are only as good as your people. They know people don't really buy products and 'stuff'; they buy people."

These leaders walk the talk. They do what they say, they lead by example and all have a desire to see each team member rise to be the very best they can. And they will compensate them generously for it.

Greg also identifies another important characteristic they all seem to have. "That's an insatiable need for knowledge and personal growth. These business owners are continually reading any non-fiction book or listening to programs to help them learn more. They think nothing of attending various seminars and courses run by top speakers, trainers and mentors. It still amazes me how sceptical and cynical the average business owner is out there about this and, of course, it rubs off on their team and ultimately their customers.

"They believe marketing is an investment and that customers should be turned into Raving Fans," he continues. "In fact the whole team is trained how to keep customers for life and how to generate business through referrals. These people are never scared of giving something new a try, as long as the results are known and reviewed. We call this Test and Measure. They keep changing their approach until they get the results they desire.

"Lastly, they all have a vision to contribute – to give something back to their community, their team, their family, their customers, or to charities."

One man gives freely, yet grows all the richer; another withholds what he should give, and only suffers want [Proverbs 11-24]. Or as John Bunyan said, he who bestows his goods upon the poor shall have as much again, and ten times more.

Many people are bogged down, blaming others for their situation. They may be living in the past due to bad experiences or sitting comfortably in denial. These people, Greg say,s are uncoachable, and I agree. And they'll remain uncoachable until they make a conscious decision to take ownership of their lives. It all comes down to being able to take a simple decision – and that's a decision to be outstanding. Or as Pat puts it, to decide to mix with successful people who also have a good positive outlook on life and a positive energy which rubs off on others.

But let's now hear Steve McDonald's views about what it takes to succeed in business.

"You know, what I've found is that all sorts of people succeed in all sorts of businesses. When I look at what sets apart those that make it (and by that I mean reaching their own goals in the business) then I notice one or two common traits. Firstly, most people I work with who become truly successful are passionate about what they do. That's not to say it's the only thing they think of or that their whole life is focussed on it. It means they think about it, they talk about it, they learn about it - they really are excited about doing whatever they do really well.

Secondly, every one of them is willing to learn. They know they don't know it all. And they don't expect me to either. They accept that there is a chance to learn something from almost everyone, and they actively look for opportunities to expand their knowledge every day. One other thing, they all know that the fruit grows on the ends of the limb, and you've got to step out onto the thin end if you're going to get the real growth and rewards. It might be a bit scarier out there, but that's where real success waits."

▌ Business Coaching: The Results Speak For Themselves

"Turnover is up by 12%, and profit up by 600%.
The business is now cashflow positive."
– *Tim Roberts, The Club Shoppe.*

"Since the start of coaching, turnover has increased by 300% and profit by a
whopping 600%. Future targets exceed even that."
- *Scott Paterson, First Choice Protective Coatings.*

"One thing we have insisted on is that as each franchisee comes on board, they
get a Business Coach for at least 3 months to ensure their success. I would
recommend this as a must for any franchise out there. Working with **ACTION** has
been incredible for the business. Every business owner should take it up because it
is an investment in his or her own knowledge and skill."
– *Ken Lee, Health Information Pharmacy.*

"The business doubled in turnover from $2,300 a week to over $4,000 a week
within 2 months. That's nearly a 100% increase."
– *Vance Fitzgerald, Live It Up Hairdressing.*

"For the 2001/2002 financial year, I recorded over 3 times the turnover of my
previous best year – that's a 300% increase in 12 months, and we are on target to
double that again for the 2002/2003 financial year."
– *Shane Besson, Beautiful Bathrooms of Sydney.*

"Increased my turnover by 500% in 12 months, increased my team from being a
one-man team to managing 15 people, saved over $100,000 in purchasing a
business, from no strategic alliances to having over 6 that actively refer clients,
being able to systemise my business, 90% success rate with my marketing
campaigns (being able to measure the success as well), and increased my client
base 650% in twelve months."
– *Jamie Short, Ignite Health Pty Ltd.*

Business Coaching: The Results Speak For Themselves

"What have we achieved so far? I'd say there's probably been a 15-20%
increase in number of customers we get."
– Wendy East, Café Istanbul.

"I think that whenever anyone starts a new business, they get their lawyer and an
accountant, but they should also get a Business Coach. I think that if you consider
the high attrition rate of new businesses – how many go under in the first two or
three years – I probably would also have gone under if I didn't have Steve here to
help me through. I now understand my worth – my business' worth. I've just
doubled my human resources. I now bill, and bill a good amount, for
the work that I do."
– Mary Sue Severn, Achieve! Ltd.

"Despite my apprehension at the beginning, we have achieved what we set out to
achieve and I am very please with the sales results."
- Seah King Ming, Rendezvous Hock Lock Kee Restaurant. Sales increased by 75%.

"I have benefited so much from the coaching service that without any hesitation
I would recommend it to any business owner who has a strong desire
to grow their business."
– Stephen Lee, Ridpest Sdn, Bhp. Annual turnover jumped by an impressive 60%.

"So a lot of the value that I received from coaching has been to do with
those fundamental concepts (motivation, accountability, focus and an impartial
point-of-view). At the moment I'm setting it up for the future. Revenue streams,
business tools…but basically I'm keeping the commitment with Steve because
I actually enjoy it."
– Jonathan Black, FarSight Ltd.

"I'm so much closer to my goals than most people I know. I am working towards
that and I have a plan. I'm learning how to implement all of this. I think it will all
look very different in the end."
– Angeline Knapp, Indulge Beauty Therapy Ltd.

"As for our achievements, we're now moving on again and that's critical. We've had huge growth in our customer base and because this growth is predominantly word of mouth, that's exponential. We now have more staff, which relieves us of some of the pressure, which in turn will ensure we can meet demands."
– Sarah Symon, RealSure Ltd.

"Incredibly, we have now just purchased our own new factory, office and showroom and are going to set it all up for perfect production and workflow. In fact, we will set it up now with everything we learnt from Greg and ACTION. We are all very exited about what we have achieved and what we have today."
– Pernille Lemming, DK Design Kitchens. Whereas the business previously ran at a slight loss, it has just managed to record a net profit of $250,000, with a turnover of $3 million.

"Without doubt, my twelve months with Graham strengthened my ability to be the No 1 franchisee within Harvey Norman."
– Glen Gregory, Harvey Norman Computer Store. In only eight months he grew his turnover by nearly 18%, from $9.2 million to over $11 million, and raised the profit from 10.1% to nearly 17%.

"I think we are doing the right things to turn things around and to make an incredible success story. I can now tell you exactly how many leads we need each month to break even for the month and how much profit I will make for each additional lead. After working with Eric, our conversion rate has tripled from 11% to a whopping 41%."
– Chad Longenecker, The CHAD Group, Inc.

"Coaching really got us out of the mud. Before we were in the dark, now we can see. Since starting coaching we've had a 65% increase in sales in the 12 months to the end of June, with an even better profit result. And this has been in a very competitive market that is going through a cyclical downturn with some businesses still closing down."
– Bill Ruddle, Taplin Security Products.

■ ABOUT THE AUTHOR -

Bradley J Sugars

Brad is an entrepreneur for many reasons. By the time he was just 28 years of age he was the International Chairman of a global franchise that he started with NO capital. He had his first business at age 15, made a lot of money by the age of 22, lost it all by 22 ¹/2, then paid back all his debts and financially retired at 26.

At the age of 15 he employed his friends as paper delivery boys and gleaned a few dollars for the papers they delivered. Since then his businesses have become a little more sophisticated, yet still based on the same principle of finding something people want to buy then selling it to them, making sure he charged well, and gave great service.

By the time he'd finished University, he had completed a Bachelor of Business-Accounting and worked in 27 different jobs; from gardener to pipe maker, pizza cook to radio announcer, and disc-jockey to accounts clerk. One thing he'd definitely learnt; very few people ever really gave anything their best.

As soon as he'd left Uni he got a job selling and invested every single dollar he earned into training himself. Courses on money, investing, sales, business, personal growth - you name it, he did a course in it. He knew that to achieve what he wanted out of life wasn't going to be about how hard he worked, but about how much he knew. By the time he was 21, he was running four retail stores and a photocopy management contract, earning a salary of $60,000 a year.

His mum almost had a heart attack when he told her that he had quit to go and work for himself. Being young and naive was probably a good thing. No capital, but a lot of smart ideas on how to create sales, how to market and how to lead a team of people. By the way, those retail stores increased profits by 39% in the nine months he was in charge.

He bought into a ladies fashion store, a 33% holding with no money down; just the ability to help them create sales. He increased sales by 93% over the first nine weeks and sold his interest back to the other partners just three months later. He did the same with a pizza manufacturing business; he took their product from just being sold into cafes and got it on the shelves of Woolworths, and almost every other small retailer in Queensland. He funded this growth with his earnings from the ladies wear store and was also doing some business consulting in his spare time.

It was this consulting that really led him to where he is today. One gentleman he offered his services to *(he used to give away two hours of his time for free, just so people could understand what he could do for them)* ran an international training company.

This gentleman, Robert Kiyosaki, a best selling author, asked him to come and train his seminar promoters in the art of marketing. Little did he know then what was in store for him.

Training 30 seminar promoters in Hawaii meant that he was bound to go into the presenting business. Seminars in Hong Kong, New Zealand and in Melbourne meant the sale of the pizza business to create an international operation training and consulting to business owners and managers. Robert asked him to train at his Business School for Entrepreneurs in Hawaii later that year. That was July 1994, and 350 business owners from around the world, 11 trainers (mostly in their 40's and 50's) were there to learn from Brad. He found a business partner who could take care of the operations back home while he got out and presented seminars, did consulting and basically generated the cashflow. And that he certainly did with hundreds of seminars, as many plane flights all over Australia, New Zealand, Asia and into the United States resulting.

He arrived home in January 1995 to find not only was he was not only tired, sick of travel, and missing regular business, but he was also broke. Major business lesson number one; partnerships don't always work. What to him was VERY serious debt caused him to move back into his parents house, get a phone line connected, put a desk next to his bed and start all over again.

He almost went and got a job. And, as he'd just spent the last 11 months teaching everyone else how to make money (and getting great results for them), he spent three full days just sitting quietly wondering why he couldn't seem to do the same for himself. At the time he thought that life could never get any worse.

He sent a letter to every one of his past clients, seminar attendees and everyone else he knew, offering his consulting services again. And, after a few solid days on the phone, he was back in business. He sat down and wrote out the Vision, Mission and Culture Statement of the new company he was going to create. He decided to stay in the business of training business owners, but this time he'd be sure to do it well.

In March of that year his best friend from University began working with him. They worked from Brad's parents' 'granny flat'. Brad recorded sets of tapes while doing the seminars, kept selling and consulting during the day, and continued selling the tapes. They stayed back until about 10 or 11 each night planning and systemising.

It wasn't long before he'd paid back everything, saved a few dollars, and had a plan in place to create an amazing worldwide organisation. To cut a long story short, within three years and after many trials and tribulations, he managed to create a company called **ACTION International.** Employing 24 people in Australia, they took care of the business in Australia and New Zealand. A joint venture deal (worth several millions of dollars) was then signed to open an office in Singapore to service South East Asia and in 1998 he took the big decision to go global through franchising. 188,000 people had attended *ACTION* seminars by then, 14,300 had been through their intensive workshops, and 397 had benefited from *ACTION* consulting services.

Brad Sugars is currently the Managing Director and CEO of *ACTION International* Pty Ltd, as well as Chairman of the *ACTION* Group of Companies around the globe.

Brad is available for a limited number of speaking engagements each year. If you are interested in booking Brad as a keynote speaker for your next annual conference or business event, call *ACTION International* on +61 (7) 3368 2525. It's literally guaranteed that your attendees will say he's "the best speaker we've ever had," time and time again.

■ RECOMMENDED READING LIST

ACTION INTERNATIONAL BOOK LIST

" The only difference between YOU now and YOU in 5 years time will be the people you meet and the books you read ..." Charlie 'tremendous' Jones

"And, the only difference between YOUR income now and YOUR income in 5 years time will be the people you meet, the books you read, the tapes you listen to, and then how YOU apply it all ..." Brad Sugars

- The E-Myth Revisited by Michael E. Gerber
- My Life in Advertising & Scientific Advertising by Claude Hopkins
- Tested Advertising Methods by John Caples
- Building the Happiness Centered Business by Dr. Paddi Lund
- Write Language by Paul Dunn & Alan Pease
- 7 Habits of Highly Effective People by Steven Covey
- First Things First by Steven Covey
- Awaken the Giant Within by Anthony Robbins
- Unlimited Power by Anthony Robbins
- 22 Immutable Laws of Marketing by Al Reis & Jack Trout
- 21 Ways to Build a Referral Based Business by Brad Sugars
- 21 Ways to Increase Your Advertising Response by Mark Tier
- The One Minute Salesperson by Spencer Johnson & Larry Wilson
- The One Minute Manager by Spencer Johnson & Kenneth Blanchard
- The Great Sales Book by Jack Collis
- Way of the Peaceful Warrior by Dan Millman
- How to Build a Championship Team - 6 Audio tapes by Blair Singer
- Brad Sugars "Introduction to Sales & Marketing" 3 hour Video
- Leverage - Board Game by Brad Sugars
- 17 Ways to Increase Your Business Profits booklet & tape by Brad Sugars. FREE OF CHARGE to Business Owners

*To order products from the recommended reading list call *ACTION International* on +61 (7) 3368 2525

Get Stacks of CASH and Heaps of CUSTOMERS ...

... get your ads designed by our Champion Creative Team ...

As you've just seen there's a lot to remember when it comes to writing effective ads. Well imagine having a team of marketing professionals design your ads for you ...

You will have some of the best in the country writing and designing your ads for you. Professionals who have created thousands of profitable advertisements and marketing campaigns.

Imagine having a Yellow Pages ad that has your phone ringing off the hook, or a Print Ad that has customers flocking through your door. Maybe you'd like an irresistible Sales Script that make prospects feel compelled to buy, or a Referral Strategy that generates hundreds of qualified, cost effective new leads. Our team of copywriters and graphic artists can give you all this and more ...

You can have our Champion Creative Team design a Web-site that will have the orders flooding in, or a Direct Mail campaign that turns your mail box into an amazing profit generating centre. If you're looking to change your image, imagine having our Champion Creative Team design your new Corporate Image or Logo. Best of all we give you a dozen variations on your ads for you to test and measure, so you can be sure to find one that gets amazing results.

Our team is not focussed on being 'clever' or winning awards. For years they've honed their skills in creating campaigns with one goal in mind ... Making Our Clients MONEY.

Being in business is not about doing it all yourself, it's about Leverage. It's about getting outside professionals doing the work for you, so your time is free to focus on growing your business and reaping the rewards. So why spend hours trying to design ads yourself, when you can have our creative team put together a sales and profit focused campaign that will have the money rolling in, in no time.

Call our team TODAY on 1800 670 335, and have us get started on your MONEY MAKING Campaign.

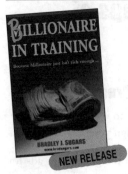

Billionaire In Training

90% of the stuff in this book is missing from most of the wealth creation manuals which are available on the market today ...

Designed to save aspiring Entrepreneurs a lot of mistakes, Billionaire In Training provides an essential framework for creating business success including strategies for increasing profit; a how-to guide for buying, selling and keeping businesses, how to keep yourself on track and moving toward your goals, the 5 Levels of an Entrepreneur and how to advance yourself to the upper levels.

AUD $29.95
(Incl. GST)

Cash, Customers and Ads That Sell

149 Hints, Tips and Strategies on writing Ads that Sell

Armed with all of Brad's super powerful advertising hints and tips, you'll be ready to write super profitable ads in no time at all ...

With Cash, Customers and Ads that Sell, you'll quickly learn how to create profitable strategies and then how to create the ads that make the strategies work ... You'd be mad to pass up the opportunity to get this book.

AUD $29.95
(Incl. GST)

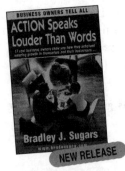

ACTION Speaks Louder Than Words

This book is about ordinary business people achieving astonishing results through business coaching. It chronicles the experiences of 17 businesses and outlines how they achieved phenomenal growth. You'll discover that the only real way to achieving amazing results for your business lies through business coaching. And you'll see it doesn't matter what type of business you run, how old or new your business is, how small or big, or even in what economy you're operating in, coaching can produce unimaginable results.

AUD $29.95
(Incl. GST)

Leverage:
The Game of Business

The rewards start flowing the moment you start playing ...

Leverage is a educational breakthrough that'll have you quickly racking up the profits.

AUD $295.00
(Incl. GST)

The principles you take from playing this game will set you up for a lifetime of business success. It'll alter your perception and open your mind to what's truly possible. Sit back and watch your profits soar.

NEW RELEASE

$ales Rich Video Series

Now you can learn the sales secrets that allowed Brad Sugars to financially retire at the age of 26. And, unlike most gurus, he started with NOTHING.

Take advantage of the only multi-millionaire who will teach you exactly how he did it. In this six-video set, Brad gives you more than just theory; he gives you practical step-by-step instructions to take you from being just an average sales person to becoming a SALES SUPERSTAR. And all for just $495.

AUD $495.00
(Incl. GST)

Billionaire In Training Video

Whether you've read the book or not, you've just got to view this video. Watch Brad Sugars in action as he fires up his audience, imparting powerful business secrets in an easy-to-understand fashion.

Not only will you find this best-selling video great value at $59, you'll find it very informative and highly entertaining. It's no wonder he's widely regarded as one of the world's leading business speakers.

AUD $59.00
(Incl. GST)

BEST SELLER

AUD $29.95
(Incl. GST)

Instant Cashflow
(Revised Edition)

Now you can learn Brad's most amazingly powerful and user-friendly sales and marketing tips all in one book.

This book will complement everything you will learn at Brad's Seminar. You will read this book once, then refer to it again and again!

There are so many simple, easy and ready-to-use tips on how to boost your bottom line that you'll have to refer it to your family and friends as well.

NEW RELEASE

AUD $29.95
(Incl. GST)

Instant Leads

One of the fundamental problems most businesses face is the generation of new leads. Without a constant supply of leads, they're faced with a never-ending battle to generate sufficient cashflow for the business to survive from one month to the next.

This book is designed to give you the inside track on everything you need to know about how to generate more leads for your business. It aims at providing you with an INSTANT guide on how to produce the various lead generation tools just like the professionals.

NEW RELEASE

AUD $29.95
(Incl. GST)

Instant Sales

By reading this book, you'll discover the secrets of selling. You'll also discover that the sales process actually starts well before you get to the stage of meeting your prospect face-to-face. You may even be surprised to discover this process actually starts with YOU.

In this book, Brad Sugars explains how to maximise your Conversion Rate, or to put it another way, how to make sure your prospects actually buy from you. He also explains some not-so-well-known techniques that are aimed at smoothing your path through the sales process.

AUD $29.95
(Incl. GST)

Instant Promotions

Brad Sugars knows a thing or two about promoting a business. Learn his secrets and follow his easy-to-understand and simple-to-implement steps to promotional success that will put your business on the map.

This book is designed to give you the inside track on everything you need to know about promoting your business. It aims to provide you with an INSTANT guide on how to produce the various promotional items just like the professionals. Once you've read the book, you'll know precisely what it takes to successfully promote your business.

AUD $29.95
(Incl. GST)

Instant Repeat Business

Hanging on to an existing customer is far easier, and much cheaper, than looking for new ones. Yet few business people realise this.

This book is all about looking after repeat business. It's all about ensuring your existing client-base remains happy, loyal and content. It's all about ensuring you look after that 20% of your customer-base that accounts for 80% of your turnover. It's all about turning your existing customers into your most prized asset – Raving Fans.

Order all your Brad Sugars' products online ...

Getting hold of Brad Sugars' books and other products is now easier than ever before. Simply log on to bradsugars.com and buy online – it's as simple as that. Bookmark this site and keep up to date with the latest information from one of the world's leading business experts.

www.bradsugars.com

■ Double or Triple Your Profits Over the Next 12 Months ...

... and actually work less than half the hours you're currently working ...

This is the most important business workshop you'll ever attend ...

Take your business, whether it's running profitably, making a loss, or even just the seed of an idea and invest 5 days learning and applying strategies that will make you a marketing master. You'll leave the program with a bunch of strategies and ideas that will have your business flying. PLUS, you'll leave with a heap of ads and letters ready to generate real cash for you the moment you get back to your business.

Over the 5 days of Brad Sugars' MARKETING OVERHAUL WORKSHOP you'll discover the most powerful formula for creating cashflow in the world of business. You'll cover more than 70 different ways to generate leads. We will show you dozens of ways to increase the response to your advertising, and actually manage to spend less than you're currently spending.

You'll discover how to increase your conversion rate. It's great to get more enquiries, but it's pointless if you don't make sales. With just a couple of simple techniques you'll be able to sell to more people, without ever needing to offer a discount, or cut into your margins.

You'll probably also like to hear the 5 easiest ways to get your customers coming back more often. I'll take a moment to show you why this one simple idea can be the difference between a business that makes money, and one that goes to the wall. Imagine being able to get each customer spending more when they come into your business. You'll get 53 different strategies, any number of which could increase your cash flow overnight.

We'll also have a talk to you about your margins. It's one thing to have a good turnover, but at the end of the day, we're in business to make money. I'll let you in on 67 strategies that we've used in the past to help business owners make more out of each sale. PLUS you'll learn how to leverage yourself out of your business so you can start working 'ON' your business rather than 'IN' it. You'll also learn how to attract, motivate and keep top class employees.

The MARKETING OVERHAUL WORKSHOP will do more than simply teach you a few marketing strategies. It will give you the mindset of success, and the tools to achieve your business goals. If you want to get ahead of the pack you MUST attend this workshop.

Places in this course are strictly limited. To reserve your place call ACTION International TODAY. *ACTION International* Australia and New Zealand +61 (0)7 3368 2525

Free call within Australia 1800 670 335

Free call within New Zealand 0800 440 335

Singapore and Asia +(65) 221 0100

United States of America (888) 483 2828

Canada (403) 259 5546

∎ Entrepreneurs Training, Where You Discover How to Make Your Wildest Dreams a Reality ...

And, here's why we won't let most people attend this training program...

Never before has there been a workshop like this. Presented by entrepreneur and marketing guru Brad Sugars, this workshop will teach you everything you'll ever need to know about personal wealth, lifestyle and business success. It will change your life in the most positive way imaginable.

The Entrepreneurs Training is not open to everyone. In fact, it's open only to those who share a common goal - the desire to succeed.

Whether you're looking to make the most of your personal wealth, or increase the cashflow of your business, this 5 day, live-in workshop, will provide you with memorable gifts that will remain with you for the rest of your life.

This workshop is strictly invitation only. You'll need more than just money and time to attend this course. You'll need to embrace the workshop's motto - 'Whatever it takes'. 100% full on from the word go, you'll work hard, play hard and learn the level of performance you'll need to work at to create the entrepreneurial success you're after ...

If you could imagine what it would be like to achieve everything you've ever dreamt of, and have 100% trust in yourself, you'll understand why the Action Entrepreneurs Training is strictly Employees Not Allowed. You can never live in a state of fear, or work from an unleveraged place again after you've lived through these 5 days ...

You don't make a fortune running businesses, you make a fortune selling them. Discover how to take every business you have and turn it into capital growth. Unlike property, shares or any other form of investment, you can massively increase the value of your investment in a very short space of time, reaping the rewards both along the way and when you sell.

This workshop will do more than simply teach you how to make money. It's about discovering who you are, and who you want to be. You're guaranteed to get more out of The Entrepreneurs Workshop than any other workshop you've been to in the past.

This workshop is an absolute must. Call *ACTION International* TODAY to reserve your place. *ACTION International* Australia & New Zealand +61 (0)7 3368 2525

Free call within Australia 1800 670 335
Free call within New Zealand 0800 440 335
Singapore and Asia +(65) 221 0100
Free call within United States of America (888) 483 2828
Canada (403) 259 5546

■ ACTION Contact Details ...

Action International **Australia**

Ground Floor, ACTION House, 2 Mayneview Street, Milton QLD 4064

Ph: 61 (0) 7 3368 2525

Fax: 61 (0) 7 3368 2535

Free Call: 1800 670 335

Action International **Asia**

171 Tras Street, #08-177 Union Building, Singapore 079025

Ph: 65 (0) 6 221 0100

Fax: 65 (0) 6 221 0200

Action International **Europe**

Office 407, MWB Business Exchange, 26-28 Hammersmith Grove, London W6 7BA

Ph: 44 (0) 208 600 1874

Fax: 44 (0) 208 834 1100

Action International **North America**

5670 Wynn Road Suite C, Las Vegas, Nevada 89118

Ph: 1 (702) 795 3188

Fax: 1 (702) 795 3183

Free Call: (888) 483 2828

ACTION Offices around the globe:

**Australia | Canada | China | England | France | Guatamala | Hong Kong
India | Indonesia | Ireland | Malaysia | Mexico | New Zealand | Phillipines
Scotland | Singapore | USA | Wales**

■ ATTENTION BUSINESS OWNERS ...
increase your business profits

Here's how you can have one of Brad's *ACTION* Business Coaches guide you to success...

Like every successful sporting icon or team, a business needs a coach to help it achieve it full potential. In order to guarantee your business success you can have one of Brad's teams as your business coach. You will learn about how you can get amazing business results with the help of the team at *ACTION International*.

The business coaches are ready to take you and your business on a journey that will reward you for the rest of your life. You see, we believe *ACTION* speaks louder than words.

Complete & post this card to discover how the team at *ACTION* can help you increase your income today...

ACTION International...Business Trainers and Consultants...
...Because being in business should give YOU more life...

Name . . . .

Position . . . .

Company . . . .

Address . . . .

. . . .

Phone . . . .

Fax . . . .

E-mail . . . .

Referred by . . . .